# Awake, Unite, Think, Save and Build the Nation

# Awake, Unite, Think, Save and Build the Nation

## ( जागो, जुड़ो, सोचो, देश बचाव और बनाव )

## (A Cryptic Introduction to Scams and Malpractices)

Adhikarla S Rao

KALPAZ

First Published, 2018

*Published by*
Kalpaz Publications
C-30, Satyawati Nagar,
Delhi - 110052
Ph.: 011-47034999, 9811692060
www.kalpazpublications.com
E-mail: kalpaz@hotmail.com
*Printed at:* G. Print Process, Delhi

**Cataloging in Publication Data—DK**
Courtesy: D.K. Agencies (P) Ltd.
<docinfo@dkagencies.com>

**Rao, Adhikarla S., author.**
Awake, unite, think, save and build the nation : a cryptic introduction to scams and malpractices = Jāgo, juro, soco, desa bacāva aura banāva / Adhikarla S Rao.
pages cm
Includes index.
ISBN 9789386397393

1. Malpractice—India. 2. Scandals—India. 3. Corruption—India. 4. Social problems—India. I. Title. II. Title: Jāgo, juro, soco, desa bacāva aura banāva.

LCC KNS4100.R36 2018 | DDC 344.5404121 23

# Contents

# Foreword

This collection of information regarding what is India by Dr.Rao, makes a worthyreading. Only an understanding of the contents of the book can give a correct appraisal of "Saaf Niyat" (साफ़ नियत) and "Sahi Vikas" (सही विकास). Only then "achchhe din" (अच्छे दिन) are possible. It appears that no sphere of Indian life, be it politics, administration, health, education, sports, business etc., is free of distortion and corruption. He has left out the judiciary and the film world, perhaps deliberately for another book. The malady is so deep rooted that one cannot think of any "achchhe din" (अच्छे दिन) coming soon. Going through all the instances cited, one wonders if there is anything good that is left in this country of Mahabharata and Ramayana. Our leaders of all hues claim that we are one of the advanced industrialised and scientific communities wanting to be recognized as a world super power but alas, all the instances cited by Dr.Rao makes one wonder where we really are.

The instances cited by Rao should have been supported by a reference or two. Perhaps his intention is to allow the readers of this book to search further whatever item that catches their eye. A list of references at the end would have added more weight and information. Perhaps Dr.Rao wants to write a more detailed book citing each of the instances with references in original. If he does that, it would help honest investigating agencies all over India to look into the dirt and see if something can be restored to normalcy.

It is said that when the decay in society reaches its peak and when one feels that all values of human life are lost, God is said to manifest in human form to save the humans (यदायदाहिधर्मस्यग्लानिर्भवतिभारत। अभ्युत्थानमधर्मस्यतदाऽऽत्मानंसृजाम्यहम् — Bhagavat Geetha). This is perhaps true. Despite all that is said, there have been some Indians who have cared and carried this country forward from the day we attained Independence. Most of them have gone unrecognized but we must believe that God sent them to help us to tide over through the difficult and unpleasant world around us. Had they not been there, one cannot imagine where we would have been today. Perhaps Dr. Rao has in mind to write another book on some of these great men and women, who despite all odds have tried their best to guide this country to its present state.

This book is not meant for libraries and book shelves but is for the 'man on the street' to quickly read and to know where we Indians are in India. Hence it is kept small and brief. It should be of interest to all those Indians who have our country at heart and what we should all do together do get rid of these maladies.

**Prof. Dr. P. Tauro**

PhD (Wisconsin)
Professor of Microbiology and
Dean, Post Graduate Studies (Rtd)
Haryana Agricultural University,
Hisar—125004, Haryana

# Acknowledgement

At the outset I express my gratitude to Professor P. Tauro, for agreeing to write a Foreword. He has taken pains to go through my book critically and give useful suggestions. Most encouraging part of his Foreword is that the book should be read by a large number of people in the interest of the nation. Indeed grateful to him.

I sincerely thank our research scholars, Mr. G. Satish, Mr. Anilkumar Moola and Mr.S. Prabu Kumar, for sparing their computers and helping in working with the computers. My special thanks are to Mr S. Satish who was of immense help in literature search sparing considerable time.

I also express my sincere thanks and happiness to Dr Dharam Singh Chopra, Retired Professor, Department of Biochemistry, Haryana Agricultural University, Hisar, Haryana and Shri M. L. Narayana, Retired Chief control officer, Central Government security printing press, Hyderabad (Telangana) for encouraging me during the compilation of the book.

# Acknowledgement

[illegible]

# Author's Preface and Introduction

Dear future reformers and hope of the nation, I earnestly solicit your understanding and follow up. Before it is too late let us awake, think and act coherently and save the nation. Not just that. We have to become a power to reckon with on the globe. This is possible only with the efforts of a huge number of people across the country belonging to various target groups. Know thyself. Know Thy Country.

The present handy book has been written after observing considerable disgust and cynicism of various target groups about the state of affairs and mis-happenings in our country. India is said to be passing through an era of uninterrupted scams. A quip on a face book posting was "No Scam Reported in the Past 72 hours"! Is our future bound to be only more and more gloomy? Is our future destined to deteriorate further and further? This cynicism was there since long and had been increasing with time. In support of this assertion a few quips and anecdotes.

1. Person "B" finds a treasure while ploughing a land bought from person "A". Person "B" goes to return the treasure to Person "A"! Person "A" refuses to accept it. And person "B" also refuses to take it back. Both go to Yudhishtar for

judgement. Even Yudhishtar was unable to give a decision and looks for help towards Sri KrishanBhagawan. Sri Krishan thinks for a while and asks the two persons to come on a particular day. On that particularly day both persons come again to Yudhishtar. This time both persons reverse their stand. Both "A" and "B" angrily claims the treasure for oneself. Yudhishtar was again rendered helpless in giving any decision and looks towards Sri Krishan and says why today they have changed their behaviour in a diametrically opposite way!? Sri Krishan says —today is the first day of Kaliyug! Now more than five thousand years have passed in Kaliyug. So one can imagine how people might have changed! The ancient prediction is that values will reach to an abysmal depth with the passage of time when almighty will intervene.

2. Persons from different countries went to almighty and each one has asked, Oh! Lord when our country is going to be better off? Lord said to everyone some time span. When our person's —Indian— turn came, Lord thought for a while and said — "Sorry, not in my life time". When the quip is narrated bringing Lord Brahma into picture, the same answer means that it is more than 10 billion years — the remaining life span of Lord Brahma.

3. A staunch atheist (non-believer in the existence of God) from another country came to India and travelled all over. On his way back some happened to ask his opinion about India. He said. "I was a staunch atheist before coming to India. Now I am returning to my country with

the strong belief that "God definitely exists". Otherwise who is running this country!?

4. Sir Winston Churchill said "Do not give Independence to India" as Indians lack diligence and integrity. Unfortunately many have started acknowledging his statement as on today i.e. we lack diligence and integrity.

5. British while leaving our country predicted that one day India would balkanize (break apart) one day. Though the country has not broken apart, there had been a fragmentation of the country into more number of states and more number of districts within a state and this process may continue further. Further there had been emergence of more number of political parties both at national and state level. Our country is still fighting to guard its borders and divisive tendencies sometimes keep cropping up. On the eve of $50^{th}$ year of Independence media has published many special articles and issues. In one of the articles a depressing assertion was, "there is no love lost if we break apart"! We are living together just because living separately involves maintenance of a separate military for everyone which is not possible apart from so many other burdens. More dangerous part is when everyone starts living independently it would be relatively easier for invaders to invade the country part by part.

6. A common man approaches God and appraises his problems. God asks, who is responsible for your problems? The man points out to someone. God calls that person for explanation. He politely

narrates his view points and points out to someone else. Like this it goes on and on till it reaches the PM! God calls PM for explanation. PM in turn narrates his predicament and points to someone below him. Like this it goes on and on and finally reaches to the same common man who complained to God!! God called the common man and asked him. Why did you vote for this person? Common man said. Oh! Lord there were two candidates contesting. One promised to give five rupees while the other ten rupees. So I voted for the person who promised ten rupees. (Those were the rates in very olden days! And Now!? It can be Rs 500 and 1000/ or even more in some crucial elections. A general feeling is around one lakh votes at least have to be purchased in every constituency. Apart from the direct cash the voters are provided with so many items for a certain period just before the elections, whose cumulative costs can be very high apart from the costs involved in campaigning. To this one has to add the Post-Election promises. That is what benefits the candidates are going to give to the voters after winning).

7. Once there was an official statement form the PM's office that for every rupee released by the Government only 20-25 paisa reaches the public. So one can imagine the total number of people involved in the process and the magnitude of cut. One PM got so much fed up with complaints about corruption that PM had simply said "it is a global phenomenon". This reflects how helpless even the person at the helm of affairs can be. Is this because of the

type of situation prevailing as mentioned in point "6" above?

8. A UN (United Nations) report strongly said that "corruption and population" are twin evils of democracy and mentioned India along with other countries. Apart from UN two international organisations — transparency international and world democracy audit have ranked the countries across the globe in relation to the extent of prevailing corruption. India's position is really embarrassing, particularly keeping in view its rich ancient civilisation.
9. At one time foreign investors got fed up with the lengthy and cumbersome procedures and corruption at numerous places in our offices. They said. They do not mind paying bribes but let it be a single window system. That is, the investors pay the expected total bribe at just one place and their work should be done at the earliest. But in India this was/is not possible. Because, there are numerous windows that need to be contacted! Even Indian corporates got fed up.
10. Once a newspaper columnist lamented that there is no sphere of human activity in the country which is not politicised. And once any sphere is politicised it is extremely difficult to depoliticise it. The same thing can be told about corruption. With time more and more spheres of human activities are getting corrupted and when once corrupted it is extremely difficult to clean the sphere. Another columnist lamented that corruption has become nearly all pervasive — "From Cradle to Grave"!

# Chapter - 1

# Electoral Controversies/ Criticisms

Probably it is quite apt that we start first discussing Electoral controversies / Corruption. Once acknowledging the heavy corruption in bureaucracy a senior VVIP remarked that bureaucratic corruption is rooted in political corruption and political corruption is rooted in electoral corruption. So who is to be blamed!?

On the globe India is the only most populous country which follows democracy. Apart from huge population – 134 crores plus(1.34 billion plus), India has a mind boggling heterogeneity and thus it is a great task to rule the country. India's mind boggling heterogeneity in brief: 134 crore plus people in the country are divided into 29 states and 7 union territories; 22 official languages and hundreds of dialects; 7 major religions apart from many faiths and cults; thousands of castes and sub-castes; many regional and national political parties etc. And the divisive tendencies are not yet over. In view of the above it is natural that there is a cut throat competition in every sphere of life. Elections are unavoidable part of democracy with everyone trying to come to power by all means. Of course the state of affairs are not the same since Independence till today. In the recent times while it may be a smooth affair sometimes, many times conducting and contesting elections has become a multi-faceted task and became a root cause for many problems. Alternatively one may say the electoral process has become a subject of high controversy because of the huge population —in other words huge electorate—and the above mentioned mind boggling, disgusting and depressing social heterogeneity.

At one time the size of the electorate was less as percentage of population as the voting age eligibility was 21 years. Later it was reduced to 18 years which has enormously increased the size of the electorate. There are many even today who feel that 21 years minimum is a better decision. Of course fortunately or unfortunately the voter turnout is not 100 percent but can be any low. In other words an election may be conducted with a much lesser number of eligible voters. And even this number is apparently divided among the total number of candidates contesting. Hence the candidate declared as won might have got a very less percentage of the total eligible voters. Suppose the voter turnout is total then the government has to incur much more expenditure and make much more provisions for the entire electorate to vote. So it becomes a much more burden on the government's exchequer.

In the last LokSabha elections ₹ 3,765(three thousand and seven hundred and sixty five) crores are supposed to have been spent. This is the official expenditure stated which comes out to be ₹ 1,375 per voter or 6.93 crores per M.P. (Member of Parliament). To this one has to add around ten crores at least/on an average which an M.P has to spend on his own to win the election. How much of this expenditure could have been minimised we do not know / have not made any effort to really calculate and take accordingly the steps. It is a general feeling among the public that either a prospective MP or an MLA have to spend a minimum of ten crores for one's election. So as we have 543 MP's the total expenditure comes out to be 54, 300 (Fifty four thousand three hundred) cores and for the 4, 120 MLA's we have in the country the expenditure comes out to be 41, 200 (forty one thousand and two hundred) crores! This may be a low estimate and the actual expenditure can be many times more as reported by media. It may vary from few crores to 300(three hundred) crores per MP/MLA depending on the situation. The next Lok Sabha elections in 2019 which is predicted to be a crucial one, the electoral expenditure on all accounts — both official and unofficial — is expected to increase drastically.

Why an MP/MLA has to spend so much of money?? Everyone knows that it is to keep the voters in good humour in more than one way apart from expenditure for advertisements, campaigns, travelling etc. Further some candidates have to give money to the party leader to get the ticket to contest the election and also give money in case one desires a portfolio after winning the election. Often it is said that it is inevitable for a political party to have power of 3M's (money, muscle and media), In case there is a necessity for manipulation or malpractices it becomes the $4^{th}$ M! The story does not end there. The candidate has to make a large number of promises to the voters –"I/ we will do all the following to all of you if you vote me/ us". One cannot escape saying that voters do demand their pound of flesh. Rather pound have to be replaced with ton keeping in view the electoral expenditure on them and the financial burden of post-election promises. If one contestant and political party refuses to do as above there is another contestant and political party to do as above and come to power. Such is the competition.

Now in view of the above how can anyone expect that there should be no corruption on the part of any politician/ political party?? How difficult it is for any party even voted to power to run the state fulfilling the post electoral promises made to the voters? It is simply inevitable that corruption permeates into all sectors during the tenure of 5 year period. And with every succeeding election the expenditure, electoral promises and spread and magnitude of corruption increases. While making money the politician /political party also keeps in mind the next elections. It is simply not possible for the election commission or any other authority to put a limit on electoral expenditure and punish a candidate or apolitical party for exceeding the expenditure. Because it is simply not possible to fight elections with small sums of money. Naturally large sums of money means unaccounted money or black money. It is also inevitable for them to solicit funds from businessmen/corporate sector and naturally they have to reciprocate them by due favours when the party comes to power. In case no single party emerges as the largest party to claim the formation of the government, huge expenditure is also involved in engineering defections and forming coalitions. So you can imagine how complicated the web is!?

In addition to MP's and MLA's scams and controversies are also reported from different parts of the country for the elections of MLC's (member of the legislative councils). Candidates contesting for MLC also have to spend considerable money in more than one way. In some places bribery and distribution of lures were even photographed and went viral.

A highly disturbing –but remained an unavoidable situation till now — is candidates with criminal antecedents/charges contesting and winning the elections. Roughly one third of MLA's and MP's are supposed to have criminal antecedents/ charges. And nearly one-fifth of them have serious criminal charges. It is really an incomprehensible situation. We even listen to candidates remaining in the prison contesting elections and winning! How to explain it? Why people vote for them? Apart from 3M's or 4 M's mentioned above there is another factor. Though these people may be considered as with criminal antecedents/charges by so many others they are considered as venerable leaders by the voters /people belonging to their respective social groups. In other words my venerable leader you consider as a criminal and your venerable leader I consider as a criminal. Why government / election commission is unable to prevent the candidates with criminal antecedents /charges from contesting elections? Needs to be pondered. Once in fact there was a move to debar candidates with criminal antecedents to contest. To the utter surprise of the nation all political parties have sabotaged that move! What does this mean?

In addition to what is mentioned above one may state some malpractices followed by the contestants. Only what is relatively benign and is of common knowledge are mentioned here:

(1) Many voters on the day of voting to their shock find that their names are missing in the voters list and hence cannot vote. How much of this is

inadvertent human error and how much is deliberate has been a debatable point.

(2) Sometimes voters to their shock find that their votes have already been casted and hence cannot vote. So apparently there had been a large scale impersonation.

(3) Another case where voters are not able to vote is that the poll timings are fixed and the number of polling days are not sufficient. Further there are also problems for voters who are remaining far away from their constituency

(4) Though it is supposed to be a secret ballot there is a general feeling that many contestants come to know as to who has voted or not voted for them. It is speculative as to how they arrive at this information.

(5) In every polling booth there are representatives of every contestant overseeing the whole process. Yet many non-permissible things happen. Something to be pondered over.

(6) In the recent times EVM's (Electronic voting machines) have been introduced replacing the old ballot paper system. However even this technology has become controversial. In view of so much of malpractices being reported regarding hacking of bank accounts, hacking of vital data bases etc people have become suspicious that even EVM's can be tampered with the help of modern science & technology. Of course impersonation is possible even with EVM's).

(7) In olden days when ballot papers were used the way of malpractices carried out were different.

In fact some TV channels have covered some of these malpractices.

As mentioned in the title and preface the idea is to give only a cryptic account of what went wrong and no effort has been made (rather intentionally avoided) to mention specifically anyone's name –individual or of a business organisation or the name of the place where something wrong has occurred. In future some others may be involved in the malpractices. The idea is not out point out anyone's affiliation but to educate and create awareness among the public as to how things can go wrong in different sectors. Hence only few incidences to serve the above purpose have been mentioned under every category discussed in the text. Under this category of electoral controversies a few are listed:

1. To fight elections as mentioned above politicians/ political parties require lot of funds. Hence it is not a surprise that out of the total funds only a small amount is duly accounted. The unaccounted money may be hidden or even found in banks. In the latter case it is obligatory for the party to reveal the details of the deposits into their accounts. Sometimes they got caught by the IT officials. Two cases of unaccounted money—one of 3 crores and another of 130 crores have made news in two different states.
2. It is not legal for elected representatives – MLA's, MP's- to simultaneously occupy a job – technically called "office of profit" – where they get paid both in cash and kind. Hence it was a surprise when people came to know from the media that several MLA's belonging to a

particular party have been disqualified as they were simultaneously holding other regular jobs. As every MLA and MP knows this stipulation it is a surprise as to why they do not take any precautions in time?

3. A saying-An optimist sees an opportunity in every calamity while a pessimist sees a calamity in every opportunity. Whenever government allocates money for welfare schemes, the former category takes full advantage of it. In all such grants as much money as possible is swindled by various officials by submitting inflated and forged bills. One such incident made a news when government has allocated a massive grant for a flood relief operation at a particular place.
4. A person belonging to a party has swindled Rs/ 600 crores from a corporation. The money was actually meant to purchase vehicles for several poor and backward class people in order to provide them livelihood. However the money was diverted for election campaign in several constituencies. This diversion involved purchase of costly transport facilities to specific people, distribution and appropriation of cash.
5. See also chapter IX "Digital/Cyber Crime"

## Chapter - 2

# Education/ Medical/ Recruitment/Commercialisation

Educational scams/money making in academic sector/ misappropriation of funds etc in academic sector also vary in their character and magnitude. It involves schools, colleges, universities, research institutes, funding agencies, education departments, apex bodies regulating institutes and education, funding agencies, appointing authorities, official bodies formed by the government for various purposes like conducting of entrance exams, admissions, appointments etc., The common designations involved in the above are : Vice Chancellor, Registrar, Controller of examinations, Finance officer(comptroller), Deans, Directors, Secretaries, Chairman, Vice-Chairman, Principals, etc., apart from administrative staff at various levels and political interference. Of course even faculty at various levels in the above institutes may be involved. For state universities education minister is designated as Pro-Chancellor and Governor of the respective state as Chancellor. Officially it is the Governor who is the appointing authority for the vice-Chancellors for state universities while for central universities it is the president of India who is called

"Visitor" of the university. The magnitude of money amassed varies apart from other irregularities. All the above is apart from large scale commercialisation of education by private colleges and universities. Private institutions are run by a wide category of people-Entrepreneurs, Godmen and Religious institutions, family members or someone else on behalf of politicians, bureaucrats etc. Other private enterprises involved are coaching centres and tuitions by faculty.

Long back Shri Jawaharlal Nehru said "if universities are discharging their duties well, all will be well with the country and the society". He also popularised the concept of "scientific temper'. Recently Bill gates said "one of the factors which is holding back India is the education system". Apparently till today all is not well with the education system. And in view of its vital importance as stated by Shri Jawaharlal Nehru, anything wrong in the education system must be viewed in all seriousness and is of great concern requiring remedial course of action at the earliest. It is really unfortunate that something serious happened /happens in the country in the education system too which has/have attained the level of being termed as scam/scandal etc.

1. Till today VYAPAM(an acronym) scam stands as one which has received not only national attention but also international attention as the most frightening scam.. VYAPAM is a body to conduct entrance exams for various jobs and for admitting students into medical courses. It is a large scale scandal involving wide categories of people Viz; low and high profile politicians, bureaucrats, businessmen, school teachers, invigilators, doctors, parents and guardians, students, middlemen, musclemen,

helping hands and resource persons from various places, coaching centres etc. All these categories formed an incredible nexus and adopted every possible method ultimately leading to amassing of wealth, fraudulent recruitment to jobs, fraudulent admissions to medical colleges and most unfortunately to several murders and mysterious deaths.

2. While medical admissions in VYAPAM are called as scam it is not called so in private medical colleges.(Of course in private medical colleges there is no so much of nexus and crime as above. Only money matters). Commercialisation of medical education is enormous. According to one newspaper report, professional education is one of the largest black money generator in the country amounting to about ₹ 40 thousand crores. Of this 12 thousand crores are because of medical education. The columnist did not give a complete split up of professional education. One can presume that the rest of the money is because of other professional courses like dental, engineering etc. As the author used the term "Professional Education" one has to infer that commercialisation in arts and science colleges — which are in huge number — has not been taken into calculation while quoting the figure of ₹ 40 thousand crores. If this money is included the above figure would be still higher. In a private medical college also some students may be as poor in their merit as in VYAPAM. Recently it has been reported that candidates who have got zero and even negative marks have been admitted into private medical institutes. One can imagine

the money involved in such admissions. Leave aside the quality of training imparted in private medical colleges and the quality of doctors coming out of these colleges, how about their mind set? Does it not undergo any unpredictable alterations? Don't they reflect how their parents have got so much money to pay for them? Don't they know how much money they have paid and for how much money they got the receipt from the college? How many parents of the above candidates have been under IT (Income Tax) scanner? How many of these colleges have been in trouble because of IT officials / economic offenses wing? At least after growing in their age don't these students ponder over these things?

3. Originally in Tamil language there were half a dozen movies pertaining to medical scams. Strangely no such movies were made in other sectors of education. (Of course both in Tamil and in other languages there were many movies showing various criminal activities and nexus between a don, musclemen, politicians, bureaucrats, business men, police, judiciary etc. In different movies different nexus are shown. Most embarrassing part is high profile politicians being at the mercy of the villain/ don!).

4. Fake drugs — it is very unfortunate to listen to the fake drug market in India. The adulteration of the drugs is of varied nature. Such drugs may simply turn out to be ineffective or can prove to cause more harm. In either case the patient's treatment is prolonged and has to incur more expenditure. A joke is — a person

who wanted to commit suicide consumed poison. But he did not die. Because the poison was adulterated! The extent of fakeness in India is stated differently as:

(a) 35 % of fake drugs sold all over the world comes from India whose value is around ₹ four thousand crores. Some sources quote even up to 75% which can be traced to India.

(b) 20 to 25 % of the drugs sold in India are fake and in certain regions it can be even one-third of the total drugs.

(c) Medicines for cold, cough and headache are mostly fake or of poor quality

(d) Different analysts say fake drugs may range from 12 to 25 % of the total medicines. While some try to distinguish fake and poor quality drugs others do not distinguish but add up and quote the figure.

(e) ASSOCHAM predicts that Indian fake drug market has crossed ten billion dollars. One can imagine how callous we can be to our own fellow citizens. Further as we export a lot of medicines India's image also is being gradually destroyed.

5. Other fake products— there are a huge number of other fake products. Adulteration of either drugs or any other products cannot be done by totally naive people. It requires some knowledge of the products and adulterants. So apparently some educated /technically qualified people are involved. Once it was said that adulteration has become so rampant that there is a severe shortage of adulterants and therefore even the

adulterants have to be further adulterated to meet the total requirement of adulteration!

(a) Food adulteration-another adulteration harmful to the society on a daily basis /in the day to day life is the adulteration of various food products. Food adulteration in India is supposed to have assumed epidemic proportions. Even common items consumed in the day to day life by common people like milk, ice cream, oil etc., are adulterated. Recently we had been listening to novel methods of adulteration of rice and is called plastic rice.

(b) Agricultural inputs — In spite of knowing that a huge population of 134 crores have to be fed, agricultural inputs like fertilisers, pesticides, fungicides, seeds, growth regulators etc., are adulterated. Because of these farmers have to suffer crop losses or incur more expenditure by resorting to application of much higher dose of fertiliser or paying a higher price for the unadulterated inputs. Use of adulterated inputs lead to contamination of soil and crop — edible and non-edible portions. In many crops pesticide or fungicide residue remains on the edible portions. Artificial ripening of fruits using chemicals is another widely adopted unapproved practice.

6. Kuppam Scam—an university happened to confer thousands of fraudulent higher degrees — PhD's and MPhil's that too by distance education mode amassing wealth by many. Apparently in this scam also many are involved.

7. Though the VYAPAM and KUPPAM scams are very often quoted because of their magnitude at a single place, cumulatively various malpractices and money making in educational institutions of all categories across the country is likely to be more compared to the above scams.

   It is quite common for news items to appear regarding irregularities, corruption etc pertaining to both academic and non-academic sector. In the above are implicated various people at helm of affairs and also lower officials. Malpractices pertain to a wide range of matters viz; appointments, promotions, transfers, giving contracts of various items –minor to major—to various individuals/firms, severe financial audit objections etc. Recruitment scams implicating both individuals, official bodies and specific study centres are often reported.

   In academic sector there is another major dimension; that is of conducting of examinations and evaluation of examination (answer) papers. Here irregularities and malpractices can occur at different levels Viz; question paper leakage involving both Government institutions, Private institutions and specific study and coaching centres, both poor invigilation in examination halls, fixing examiners for evaluation, wrong evaluation both intentionally and because of lack of commitment and calibre of the examiner—wrong evaluation may lead to either boosting/increase in the number of marks which a candidate gets or in not getting the duly deserving marks by the candidates, manipulating the marks while computerising the data, re-evaluation of answer papers etc. Large scale manipulation of marks by re-evaluation of answer papers has recently been reported in a prestigious university.

Another inherent problem in the awarding of final marks to a candidate is the different modes of evaluation being approved by the Government and the government apex bodies. They allow internal evaluation i.e by the concerned course teacher in the respective institute. This can vary from 25% to 100 %. In very olden days the entire answer script for 100 marks were evaluated by an external examiner.. Now it is as above in general. While there can be some control in Government institutions it is not possible to monitor the private institutes.

Cumulatively all the above amounts to a huge amount of money making at different levels. In an academic sector naturally academicians/ teachers also get involved. However even if an academician/teacher is honest there still goes on what all that is mentioned above at other levels. Either in academic sector or in non-academic sector suspension or dismissal or even a short imprisonment may not affect much the individual as the individual has made sufficient money by that time. Any malpractice, scam, scandal etc does not immediately come to the surface but only after a long period. By that time so many might have made enough money and took all precautions to safeguard themselves.

Private educational institutions have their own stakes. And most of them are affiliated to

Government Institutes. It is not that easy for Government Institutes to withstand them.

Of late plagiarism and predatory (fake) journals have become a big issue in academic sector. Large scale plagiarism and large number of fake journals which publish the research work of PhD students and other researchers for money have been reported in the country. It is sad to know that India is one of the hubs for fake scientific journals. Money involved is huge enough to call it as scam. Of course the whole issue is more complex, as India has a vast education system with nearly 900 Universities, 40, 000 colleges and 400 research institutes. Funds for the above are very much limited but research outcome is expected from so many. It is extremely difficult to monitor.

8. Many parents using many means to pass their children in exams or to secure more marks in exams are not uncommon across the country. But rarely does it make news.
9. A senior official of an apex body was involved in a bribery case of ₹ two crores for approving a professional college. This is in fact a very common phenomenon with all categories of professional colleges and also private non-professional colleges. The general feeling is, irrespective of whether a college fulfils the requirement or not the bribes have to be given. However another general feeling is, in general colleges do not fulfil the requirements. Neither apex bodies nor parents and students are worried about the state of affairs in a college. They just want to have a degree. Rarely action is taken.

10. In a rural health improvement programme a scam of Rs/five hundred crore was reported.
11. In two government dental colleges several equipments at inflated prices were purchased. This scam was estimated to be of several crores.
12. Every year nearly 7 million women are estimated to be undergoing abortions of which 56% are unsafe. Both legal and illegal abortions take place. Both formally qualified and quacks may be involved in carrying out the abortions.
13. A huge number of people resort to alternative and complementary systems of medicine. We even have a ministry for the same — AYUSH indicating Ayurveda, Yoga, Unani, Siddha and Homeopathy. Many intellectuals and formally qualified people disapprove the above systems of medicine as they are not scientifically validated and consider the practitioners as pseudo. In some foreign countries the above systems are not covered under medical insurance schemes. In spite of all the above at least two systems, Ayurveda, and homeopathy are flourishing and many people have confidence in them. Even in these systems malpractices have been reported. An Ayurveda scam of ₹ 32 crore was reported form a particular state. Modus operandi was a VIP managed a greater budget to the Ayurveda department and misappropriated funds in the supply of medicines and medical kits. Some medicines were even sold at much inflated rates. Another strong suspicion about the above systems is the availability and supply of various medicinal plants in required quantities. So even these

medicines are probably are not as specified by the tradition.

14. In all sectors many controversial appointments starting from lowest level to the highest level are common. Cash, all 'isms' i.e. nepotism, casteism, regionalism, religious affiliation, linguistic affiliation, ideological affiliation, political affiliation with or without political and bureaucratic interference or support from high profile people from the society — all can play a part in the recruitments. Some recruitment make headlines. For example recruitment of several people in a steel plant and teachers recruitment in a particular state. Candidates to become teachers have to clear TET(Teachers Eligibility test) in a particular state. Candidates were promised to get passed in the test for a heavy bribe. Many resorted to it. Each candidate was supposed to have given a bribe of 2 to 5 lakhs to the people involved in the racket. Cumulatively at least 1.58 crores of rupees have been paid as bribes to different people. Similarly 355 assistant teachers were appointed in government primary schools which are exclusively political appointments. Illegal recruitments involved 350 relation executives (RE's) and 1,250 business associates (clerks) have been reported in a particular state. No recruitment details of the recruitment process was made public across the nation though may be known locally in that state.

15. In a particular state so many educational institutions were involved in amassing ₹ one thousand crores from the funds meant to give scholarships to various categories of poor

students. Over the years each institute benefitted to a different extent. The manner of illegal ways adopted was shocking. There were no students existing but scholarships were taken in fake names or very few students really existed. And the vast majority were fake. Often the scholarships were claimed on the same names of the students but from different districts of the same state. Even fake colleges were there. In a nutshell total number of students benefitted were negligible than the number of students who were to be benefitted by the government allocated money.

16. The above type of scam i.e. scholarship scam took place in some other states too. In one state scholarship amount sanctioned by social welfare department was swindled. To the extent of ₹ 50 crores. The height of swindling was that the scholarships were shown to have been distributed to non-existent colleges, schools and students. Seized property from the accused includes five houses, 18 apartments, 12 commercial buildings, six cars, gold and jewellery, cash and 287 acres of farm land.

17. A large number of educational institutions have swindled thousands of crores of rupees which were earmarked by a state government towards scholarships of various backward categories of students. Officials involved with the various institutes —apparently in connivance with the social welfare and tribal department—adopted various tricks to swindle the money, like giving scholarships to non-existent students, giving scholarships to students in courses which are not approved for availing the scholarships,

giving only a small percentage of actual scholarship amount to the students with the rest being put in the institutions account etc.

18. In yet another state just in one particular district the government found that 20% of the students being shown to the government were indeed not studying in schools funded by the government. In some sections there were no students at all. The money which should have gone towards these students expenditure was ₹ 120 crores. This is just in one district. Subsequently such anomalies were apparently found to varying extents in other districts of the state.

19. Students not on rolls and even teachers not on rolls, non-existing buildings and roads also have been reported in different parts of the country as if they were existing. Even salaries were being paid to these non-existing teachers and were shown on records.

20. In view of the above points from 14 to 18 how do you consider this anecdote /quip? Once our VIP went to another country. There he was invited by the VIP of that particular country to his house. Our VIP was highly excited looking at the lavishly built and equipped house of the foreign VIP. Our VIP asked the foreign VIP. Hey, how did you manage to construct such a house? Foreign VIP took our VIP to a balcony and asked, do you see the bridge over there at a distance? Our VIP said yes. Foreign VIP replied, you see ten percent of the total cost of the bridge was mine! Next time the foreign VIP came to India and visited our VIP's house. Same sequence of dialogues took place but

with a difference. When our VIP asked do you see the bridge over there at a distance? Foreign VIP replied 'no' because there was no bridge visible. Our VIP coolly replied 100 % of the cost of the bridge is mine!!

21. Governments institute many types of social welfare schemes and almost all of them end up in controversy. A sum of ₹ 206 crores ear marked for child development services was misutilised by indiscriminately awarding contracts to various people to cater to the needs of child development services.
22. Recently leaking of CBSE(Central Board of Secondary Education) has hit the headlines and reported as a scam. Initially the leakage of questions papers of economics and mathematics of 12th and 10th class respectively was reported but subsequently suspicion —rather almost certain— arose for the leakage of biology and accountancy papers of 12th class. Rumours were also there for the leakage of Urdu paper also. Coaching centres, school teachers and others are supposed to be involved in the scam. Many students also got involved in receiving and /or passing on the leaked papers. The papers also had access to officials of both teaching and administration. As the leakage has not percolated to all students from those places where papers were not leaked pleaded with the CBSE/MHRD not to conduct any re-examination for them but confine the re-examination only to those places where the papers have been leaked. Each student was supposed to have paid Rs/2000-2500 for getting access to the question paper. The problem

seems to be a serious one in view of a high profile person saying that "Mafia in education system seems deeper than even the coal mining industry with reference to CBSE paper leakage". As CBSE is a big network of 20,299 schools the government to avoid such incidences in future has taken the technological support of the Microsoft company. With the technology developed by them now question papers will be leak proof till 30 minutes before the start of examination. In case the papers are leaked before 30 minutes the leak can be traced (tracked) with the help of the technology developed by the Microsoft.

23. It is not only CBSE papers but leakage of question papers of the entrance exams to various degree courses in different parts of the country is not uncommon. Rarely one or other gets caught and even dismissed from the services. But that may not bother them in case they have made enough money in the process of leaking the question papers. In fact it is so with the accused/convicts in other scams. Either dismissal or even a short prison sentence does not bother them in case they have made enough money. Law enforcing agencies are seldom able to recover the money, partly if at all. Still enough is there for the convict to enjoy after his sentence is completed.

24. Points 21 and 22 should be viewed as follows. In any large scale common entrance exam the process inevitably involves so many people. Papers have to be set by examiners, rechecked, typed and may involve translation from English to vernacular, given for printing, have to be

stored till the date of exams and then distributed to various centres etc. Hence many people are involved and theoretically any one or more of the above can be involved in the leakage of papers. With so many people getting involved possibilities of leakage are very high though every time it does not make a news.

25. Many ills plaguing the Indian university system have been pointed out in the 41st Indian social science congress at Periyar University, Salem, Tamilnadu. Papers and abstracts of the publications have been published. As per February 2017, there are supposed to be 789 universities, 37,204 colleges and 11,443 stand-alone institutions as per the UGC information. Obviously with such a large educational system the prevalence, type and magnitude of ills reported as felt by the people and students working in the above institutes vary. Some of the key expressions and Key words expressed as a matter of concern in the congress were as follows:

    (a) highly inadequate working days in an academic year and inadequate working hours per week.

    (b) Highly inadequate funds and highly skewed distribution of funds.

    (c) Lack of uniformity in rules and regulations —in relation to various aspects — as higher education is a concurrent subject and universities enjoying autonomous status. Salient key words of the various presentations were: teacher absenteeism; plagiarism; irregular mode of recruitments and promotions; brain drain; commercialisation of education; low quality education; social relevance; reforms in examination system; analysis of recommendations of various committees; value education and value added education; political and bureaucratic interference; under employment/ unemployment/ unemployability; comparison with other educational systems in the world; agricultural problems; make in India; adequate monitoring and evaluation of various activities; large scale emergence of coaching centres and private tuitions, student and staff unrest; mushrooming of low quality institutes both in private and public sector; revision of acts and statutes; skewed ratio of faculty — -administrative staff — students; unmanageable number of affiliated colleges to an university; too much of bureaucracy; problems with the apex bodies; lobbies/coteries; industry – institutional collaboration; entrepreneurship etc.

26. In the $40^{th}$ Indian social science congress-coupled with Mysore(Mysuru) university (Karnataka) centenary celebrations, 2016 has discussed the theme of Bioethics very extensively and critically by many eminent professional doctors. Salient key words of the various presentations were : commercialisation of medical education; unaffordable cost of health care; lack of medical security for most of the citizens by the government; poor facilities in government hospitals; corporate hospitals;

unapproved clinical trials; organ trading; alternative/ complementary systems of medicine; high inadequacy of rural health care; consultation fees of doctors; illegal abortions; unwarranted surgeries; surrogate mothers; IVF(in vitro fertilisation) and test tube babies; side effects of various drugs; ill effects of alcohol and tobacco etc.

## Chapter - 3

# Demonetisation, Loan Defaulters, Bank & Ponzi schemes and controversies

When ₹ 500/ &₹ 1000/ notes were demonetised many honest people did put to inconvenience as the ATM's were either empty or dispensing only little amount and they were to stand in long queues both in the bank and at the ATM. Many have to request the business people to purchase items on credit. Of course some were able to utilise their credit or debit cards. Where even before demonetisation online/ electronic transactions were common people have not felt the trouble so much. In some places large number of daily wagers have lost their employment as employers were not able to or did not want to pay cash at such a time.

As on today everyone knows. It is official. Nearly all the demonetised notes have returned to RBI.Obviously no black money! Everyone was successful in converting their black money into white. And there is not going to be any further action in this regard. That is to investigate how nearly all the notes have returned to RBI. This is also certain. Even fake notes have been found to be negligible. RBI seems to have decided to destroy the demonetised notes of rupees 500 and 1000. In view of the above facts many feel it's not required— rather unwise. Better put all the demonetised notes back into circulation. If the demonetised notes are put back into circulation, people's and business establishments cash dealings in day to day will become far easier than now. Further banks will not face any cash crunch. In addition expenditure for destruction of the old notes also is saved. Presently people are feeling the absence of thousand rupee notes. Hence many feel to save the demonetised notes.

Within 53 days (one report says 23 days) after demonetisation fake 2000 rupee notes started circulating! According to the National Crime Records Bureau's (NCRB) latest report released on November 30, a total of 2,272 fake notes of Rs 2,000 denomination were seized in 2016. Since the Rs 2,000 note — along with the new Rs 500 currency — was introduced only after November 8, 2016, it means that those counterfeiting the notes got into the act very quickly. Fake Rs 2,000 notes have been reported entering India through Bangladesh, three months after the newly minted banknote was introduced.Once Border Security Force (BSF) patrol seized a bundle of 100 counterfeit notes that was thrown across the fence for "miscreants" waiting on the Indian side. The criminals escaped, leaving behind the bundle.NIA says fake Rs 2000 notes 'identical to the original'.

People got very much upset in view of the recent information about loan defaulters and the role of various banks and them becoming controversial. However one must know that though suddenly several loan defaulters have come into picture such loan defaulters and the banks who have advanced loans were there earlier also. Banks were controversial earlier also.

In a nut shell. Many banks were involved apart from facilitators. A defaulter might have cheated more than one bank or in other words many banks have given loan to the same person apparently without critically examining his past credentials. Of course each bank gave different amounts of loan. Accomplices from both within and from outside the banks are involved. Further the loan defaulters may have as accomplices their own family members, relatives, friends, co-businessmen etc. Loan defaulters often use money for purposes other than that for which loan has been sanctioned. They may divert the money into other business ventures. Hence the name of the scam does not necessarily indicate that the whole loan has been spent towards it nor it indicates that the whole scam money has been given as a loan from a single bank. The name of the scam may indicate the origin of the loan or the business establishment to which the loan was initially sanctioned. Hence one has to read/ know in detail about the loan defaulters regarding their origins of loan and utilisation of loans. There are different ways by which loan defaulters manage with the banks. Say for example—initially establishing credibility with the banks and at an opportune time the person takes a heavy loan and become a defaulter and a launderer; manage the banks because of their nexus with powerful persons in the society; keeping the banks in dark for longer time by fake documents etc.

An abstract of the loan defaulters is as follows. As on September 30, 2017, people or companies owe more than Rs 1.1 lakh crore to banks. They are not insolvents but intentional defaulters. Nationalised banks (excluding SBI and associates) constitute about 60% of this money while SBI and its associates account for one-fourth of the total. Private sector banks have declared over Rs 14,000 crores. The above amount might have still increased. In the list of defaulters each of the top 11 defaulters has loans of over Rs 1,000 crore, cumulatively amounting overRs 26,000 crore to be paid to the banks. Nationalised banks (excluding SBI and associates) constitute about 60% of this money. SBI and its associates account for one-fourth of the total. Private sector banks have also declared over Rs 14,000 crores. The above amount of 1.1 lakh crores is not an overnight phenomenon but has been accumulated over the years—rather decades. The incomprehensible fact is, in spite of banks suffering from so much of debts still they continued to give loans to people and companies! Therefore it is not a surprise if the above mentioned figure of 1.1 lakh crores further increases as there are no orders of any blanket ban issued regarding the granting of loans.

It is not an easy task as ours is a time consuming system to take any punitive action and recover all the money from all the loan defaulters. Further it is also reported in the media that some loan defaulters have quit the country. Bringing them back to our country depends on the relations we have with the other country. This is again a burden and an uncertain thing. Even if the person is brought back, it can take long time before any action is taken on the person and the money recovered. The concept of 'Justice delayed is justice denied" is not so relevant in our system which is time consuming. During the long process of investigation there can be a large number of changes in the political set up, bureaucratic set up and in the bank hierarchy. All these make the task of punishing the loan defaulter and recovering the money extremely difficult.

Loan defaulters are there not only in corporate sectors involving large sums of money but also are there –say for example in agriculture sector. The outcome of these loan defaulters can be different. The respective governments and also the general public may take a lenient view and even waive off the loans of the farmers. Cumulatively this may be considerable. In fact "waiving of loans" to farmers is one of the electoral strategies to win elections. However among farmers there can be many who take loans from private money lenders and some of them who are unable to payback commit suicides—a major issue in agriculture. It is also surprising as to why these farmers are not able to get loans from public sector banks but have to resort to private money lenders? Why the government is not generous to them who require small loans but are ready to give enormous amount of loans to others without being assured of the returns?

It is necessary in the above context as to what is a 'Ponzi" scheme/ scam? The term 'Ponzi" is not the name of any single scam but refers collectively to a category of scams/frauds. The term was derived from Charles Ponzi who first used certain strategy to cheat during 1920's. Hence the concept of Ponzi scams/schemes is not new but the surprising thing is people/companies are still able to adopt such strategies even today successfully. The cheating strategy by the operator primarily involves returns for older investors from the income of new investors. No legitimate business need to go on. When the income from new investors stops or comes down the operator does not pay anymore to the old investors but makes an escape with whatever money he could accumulate till then. A disturbing information according to SEBI (Securities and Exchange Board of India) there were/are many Ponzi type operators in India who have swindled thousands of crores of rupees cheating many investors.

It is the weakness of human psyche that is exploited. Many are tempted to have quick money/ fast buck and so they are tempted to gamble. That is where Ponzi operators succeed.

1. A Ponzi scam swindling around,₹ 3, 700 (three thousand seven hundred) crores from about 7 lakh people. This is rated as one of the biggest internet scams or social network scams or on line scams. (In olden days there was no internet though Ponzi schemes were there. What is Ponzi is explained above). The operator has promised to pay Rupees Five per every click on "like" on the web link up to a maximum of Rs/ 625 per day. That comes out to be 125 clicks per day. However the operator played a trick here. He asked everyone who wish to participate in the scheme to initially deposit Rs/5,750. As some investors start getting money many more invested. One day it all stopped. The operator along with the accomplices both from his family and outside the family have laundered the money and subsequently got investigated.

2. A financial company promised high rates of interest to the investors and even gave them post-dated cheques. Later all the cheques got bounced and investors could not encash. Investors lost one hundred crores. Four people who were former employees of a bank were booked.

3. Basic concept is the same only goods and services change. Both due to ignorance and in spite of knowing the Ponzi people continue to get trapped—

just an irresistible temptation to make money. The operator floated a bird rearing business of an Australian bird (which cannot fly) called "Emu". Hence this scam is also referred to as Emu scam. People were falsely informed about the high economic value and returns of the bird in various ways. The operator along with the promise an income of nearly 1.44 lakh within two years also has promised to return the investors deposit of ₹ 1.5 lakhs at the end. So it was just irresistible for many. Between 10 to 12 thousand people have invested — each 1.5 lakhs. Ending of the scheme is like any other Ponzi scheme and the total value of the scam was estimated to be 150 to 500 crores. Investors have to ultimately abandon the rearing of birds.

4. Once a person started five schemes in which people are promised a quick doubling of their money in investments. Nearly 92 thousand have responded and the total investments reached nearly Rs/1000/ crores. Like in other Ponzi schemes one day investors have found that have lost their money and sought police help. Like in all other Ponzi schemes a certain small number of investors did get benefitted as initially promised by the operator. And why the operator has fulfilled his promise with some? It is just to attract more number of investors—a basic methodology of Ponzi schemes. The above scamster has diverted the money to other enterprises like agriculture, electronic equipment etc., and saved cash in 61 banks. Law enforcing agencies have recovered this money and also the money from agents and promoters concerned with the above five schemes. From this money depending on which of the above schemes people have invested, different number of investors have subsequently got back anywhere from 25 to 100% of the money.

Subsequently law enforcing agencies reported that nearly 22 thousand crores of invested money is licked in various Ponzi type "increase your investment" schemes. Strange people do not learn anything from the past and from others before going ahead!

5. Role of banks in case of loan defaulters and the manner in which loan defaulters operate and the magnitude of their scams are very much different from Ponzi schemes. In view of many reports in the media of massive loan defaulters in quick succession recently everyone got little more concerned about banks and loan defaulters including all officials in the state and the nation. An abstract of loan defaulter is mentioned above. Let us look at few examples:

(a) A person and his associates have borrowed a massive loan of ₹ 40 thousand crores form a private bank and became a defaulter.

(b) Another defaulter cheated several banks cumulatively to the tune of ₹ 7 thousand crores. Each bank suffered losses to varying extent.

(c) A pen manufacturing operator subsequently emerged as one of the biggest loan defaulters, owing 3,695 crores to several banks. Like with many other scams here also the operator has got the loan from the banks by producing fake and forged banks. Loan cornered was diverted to for other purposes and in these diversions also the operator has violated many rules. The scam involves operations both from within the country and different foreign countries.

(d) Recently several bank officials were booked for a loan fraud case amounting to ₹ 600 crores during a period of four years.

(e) A firm has become a loan defaulter for a consortium of banks and financial institutions from whom loans to the extent of ₹ 40 thousand crores has been illegally taken. One single bank happened to grant a loan of Rs 3,250 crores, 86 % of which is unpaid.

(f) An hitherto well established person who was a boss of a firm was successful in defrauding a bank to the extent of 11,260 crores. This is supposed to be the biggest fraud detected till date by a single Indian bank. Subsequently the person fled from our country. Of course he is not the only person who has fled out of our country

(g) An official body concerned with urban development was supposed to have arbitrarily sanctioned loans to several individuals and corporate houses to the extent of 14,500/ crores. How much of this is recovered and how much kickbacks were paid remains controversial.

(h) Around 52 thousand peoplc have invested money in a forex trading company. Depositors were promised high rates of interest and also a percentage of company's profits for their depositors. Highly tempting. Isn't? A high level Ponzi. Ultimately depositors were duped. The scam amount was estimated to be about ₹ 8 hundred crores. Of this 90 crores the owner of the firm has put in foreign banks

(i) A private finance company involved in the business of two wheelers has managed loans adopting all fraudulent means from several banks—both private and public—and caused a loss of Rs 200/ crores. Two puzzling facts of this scam are, while private banks have filed the cases against the company, public sector banks did not and an official of the company involved in the scam was conferred a national award!

(j) Loan defaulter amount to a public sector bank for the past three fiscal years has been estimated to be 7 thousand crores.

(k) Cumulatively at different times a person became a loan defaulter to the tune of 9,900 crores duping a consortium of 17 public sector banks. Another report says 7000 cores. The same defaulter has been reported to have diverted from his total loan 3,700 crores to a sports firm in a foreign country.

(l) A gold business man has defrauded a consortium of 25 public sector banks to the tune of 12, 000 crores by siphoning off 1,705 KG of duty free gold.

(m) Few persons from the same family dealing with diamonds and jewelleries were convicted for defrauding a public sector bank to the tune of 14,000 crores by managing fraudulent letters of undertaking. Another figure quoted is 13,500 crores.

(n) Few related persons dealing with telecom products, electronics, petroleum products etc. defrauded a consortium of banks –both Government and private —to the tune of 40,000 crores. In a single deal the person concerned seems to have got a loan of 3,250 crores from a private bank.

(o) A person has swindled a public sector bank to the tune of 6, 500 crores by managing fraudulent letters of undertaking.

As so much money with so many public sector banks is involved naturally the public of the country have suffered.

# Chapter - 4

# Sophisticated malpractices, Tax Evasion, Misappropriation of Funds and Hawala Transactions

To understand some scams one requires a great understanding of the general subject of commerce and finance apart from rules and regulations and loop holes in them pertaining to national and international trade and that of all banks and RBI. One should be thoroughly knowing the intricacies involved in commerce & finance and in both conventional and modern trade. An ordinary man cannot understand much about the modus operandi. So only subject experts can educate and awareness among the public— both ordinary and at higher level- with respect to some scams. A few such are discussed here.

1. Forex derivatives scam is one of the biggest scams amounting to approximately 25 lakh crores! (Forex derivatives are contracts to buy or sell foreign currencies at a future date). Strangely the victims of the scam were from a higher level viz; importers, exporters, shareholders & investors in big corporate houses and firms selling foreign exchange

derivative contracts. The losses to the above was caused because of 19 banks violating RBI &FEMA (Foreign Exchange Management Act) guide lines to sell forex derivatives to exporters. Both Indian and foreign banks happened to lure the exporters, corporate houses to enter into derivative contracts. The unfortunate thing that also happened was RBI did not able to investigate the contracts critically.

2. NSEL (National Spot Exchange Limited) scam. An idea which has been floated by a firm is to facilitate trading of commodities right at the spot where buyer and seller are there and directly deal with. Subsequently the concept was extended to buyers and sellers situated at different locations. Further the commodities may be stored in godowns and sold at a higher price after a certain period of time. The stored commodities may be used as such or processed and used. If processed, there are another set of people/firms who can be genuine or fraudulent. In this scheme so many invested with some investing as high as two lakhs each to get more money in return. A variety of irregularities and malpractices took place in this venture. Not only ordinary investors but even investors with business acumen invested a lot in this scheme. The end result was a big scam of Rs, 5,600 crores duping 13 thousand sellers/investors in the above firm. The investigation could not trace out a considerable portion of money involved in the scam. It is speculated that one or more of the following might have happened:

   (a) money has been transferred to foreign countries through illegal (Hawala) transactions.

(b) Money has been diverted towards real estates

(c) Money used to boost other companies

(d) Money used for political interests

(e) Money went into pockets of several personalities.

The above mentioned 'a' to 'e' may happen even in several other scams.

3. A stock broker made a history in a short tenure of 2 years. He artificially rigged stock prices by utilising funds procured from various banks, promoters of different companies and industrialists. Not only has he, even others wanted him to rig the prices of those shares which have a low value. With the large sums of money borrowed from the above he was very successful in causing an unimaginable drastic increase in the share prices of many companies. One day—to the unexpectation of others— he sold his entire ownership and borrowed money from banks and companies. This has resulted in large losses for large institutional investors, insurance companies and mutual funds. Money amassed as a result of this scam is a matter of speculation. Investigating agencies convicted him and debarred from trading in stock exchange along with 25 more people. However this debarring was never treated by scamsters as a big problem as some others on their behalf can always trade.

4. In IPO (Initial Public offer) scam financiers and market players illegally bagged retail investors shares. To start with a private bank was involved and a person opened huge number of fake

'demat' (dematerialised) accounts (a "Demat" account is an account that allows investors to hold their shares in an electronic form). Subsequently some other person also was found to control a huge number of 'demat' accounts. Though 60 to 90 crore rupees were recovered from few people, a large number of investors were yet to be compensated and the value of whole scam was supposed to be far higher. A person was supposed to have drained the banks of one thousand crores and finally was successful in manipulating 3,500 crores.

5. IT department had identified and reported 64 thousand entities who had evaded taxes to the extent of ₹ 38 thousand crores. These cases were transferred to SEBI. SEBI could not investigate and take action on all. However in one particular scam it has barred nearly 1500 entities who manipulated the stock prices of 12 listed companies. So many promoters and market operators make use of stock exchange platform thereby evading taxes and launder the black money. In another scam IT department has estimated a fraud of about 10 thousand crores across the country. A particular place became a hub for this scam. In yet another scam a single business man— initially managing animal farms— from a particular state evaded income tax of about 50 thousand crores of which 20 thousand crores was supposed to have been put in foreign banks on investigation.
6. Just during a span of three years, CAG has unearthed 10,300 plus cases of fraud related to service tax and central excise duty. A split up of the above is as follows: In central excise

there were 3,690 cases of fraud amounting to ₹ 8,497 crores and in service tax there were 6,655 cases of fraud amounting to ₹ 10,662 crores. Only a small portion of the above money could be recovered by the revenue department.

7. The 2G spectrum or second generation spectrum scam had shook the nation as high profile politicians and government officials were supposed to have been involved. Time magazine listed this Telecoms Scandal as one of the top 10 abuses of power. Till then it was ranking as the biggest scam. Understanding the Modus operandi is not easy for general public as it requires greater knowledge of the process. CAG, revealed that "2G licenses had been issued to telecom operators at throwaway prices causing a loss of Rs 1.76 lakh crore to the exchequer. Moreover, licenses had been issued to ineligible applicants who had deliberately suppressed facts, disclosed incomplete information, submitted fictitious documents and used fraudulent means for getting licenses and thereby access to spectrum. Further, licenses owners had in turn sold significant stakes to the Indian/foreign companies at high premium within a short period of time". Case took a long time and finally no one was convicted.

8. It is unfortunate that because of mis-appropriation of funds even salaried class at different levels of hierarchy suffer. A strange case of the same fraternity getting involved in filing charges had surfaced—Judiciary versus Judiciary! Officials of Judiciary nominated by CBI has framed charges against several court employees which include few retired judges as

well in a particular state. All the above were charged with the illegal withdrawal of ₹ 6.58 crores from PF (Provident Fund) account of lower grade employees serving in a district court. (b) PF scam on a much larger scale occurred in another place worth nearly 93 crores belonging to 26,400 employees working in navy. The same person was also involved in a bank scam of 5.6 crore. His money saved in several accounts has been seized but it is not known how much of the diverted money is recovered. How many employees were compensated also is not clear.

9. A few women formed a women's welfare society in a particular state. Society encouraged women to invest ₹ 3,000/. In return society has promised them loans from nationalised banks to start house hold level mushroom and dairy farming projects. Interesting thing in this malpractice scheme is both the investors and the society was making mischief. Women investors instead of utilising the loans for the purposes as mentioned above were diverting it for children's education, marriages and medical treatment of the family members. Mischief from the society's side was, it was deducting ₹ 50 thousand from each loan as processing fee and commission of bank officials and gave the rest of the loan to the investors. Women investors also have to deposit some money with the society for every loan sanctioned. Society made a lot of money in the above process. When many women were unable to pay the bank loans the fraud came to light. Strangely the society itself has filed cases

against the women investors for not paying the loans.

10. Officials of EPFO (Employees Provident Fund Organisation) and a leading construction firm at a particular place has caused a loss of ₹ 169 crores to the exchequer over a period of 4 years.

11. A broker of a stock exchange in a particular state has defrauded the public of large sums of money –nearly ₹ 200 crores. Broker opened branches in two more states. Broker promised interest of ₹ 5 thousand per lakh invested. In addition of interest they were also offered an incentive of ₹ 3,500/ and 8 grams of gold. Two thousand four hundred people have got tempted and joined the company.

12. The distinction between Private and Public/ Government was /is not absolute. At one point of time many banks were nationalise and so became public sector. Before that they were under private category. However even after that many private banks continue to exist and emerge till today. In view of the recent scams some people are once again asking the government to privatise the banks. Of course there are many who object to this also. Similarly so with insurance companies. When a person—to whom some people have given the title of first swindler -—was found in large scale fraudulent operation government has nationalised different firms under LIC (Life Insurance Corporation). This person also happened to illegally transfer money from some banks as well to start new business ventures. Similarly another person also was involved in

large scale fraud involving insurance and evasion of income tax. But as on today we have so many private insurance companies advertising themselves and luring customers in various ways. Only time has to tell how many of the above will turn out to be genuine and how many as scams in future! As insurance policies are of a long term nature it may take a long time to know about them. In fact people's awareness of these insurance companies is extremely poor and do not really have an idea as to how and to what extent their investments will be useful to them nor the insurance companies divulge all their terms and conditions to the policy taker at once. A simple thing which people should understand is the companies are run primarily for their profits – not just marginal profits but huge profits. Service motive is secondary or an attractive investment for making profits. So apparently service motive constitutes a negligible portion out of the total investments companies get from clients.

13. Computer system was hacked by few people – who include government servants as well— and the data of 14 defunct companies was utilised to fraudulently withdraw ₹ 11 crores in tax credit (Read also Chapter IX "Digital/ Cyber Crime").

14. Several diamond firms involved in the import of diamonds from different foreign countries have evaded taxes to the tune of ₹ one thousand crores. Here again a loophole in the legal system has been exploited. Diamond transactions are exempted from sales tax levy in a particular

state. So the imported diamonds were shown to be transported to addresses in that particular state. After the diamonds consignment reaches the airport of another state, with the help of clearing agents the firms got them cleared but shown as if they have been dispatched to the above state where the diamonds are exempted from sales levy. Investigating agencies detected that clearing agents were unable to show proof that the consignments were being transported from the airport of one state to the above mentioned state.

15. A large number of FIR's (First Information report) cases were lodged by sales tax department against steel traders for tax evasion. The tax evasion comes to ₹ 125 crores. These evaders resorted to all malpractices possible to evade taxes.

16. High profile officials from two different public organisations were involved in defrauding the central exchequer of nearly three crores. This money was actually to be refunded to income tax payers but was diverted to a credit society.

17. Huge financial loss of ₹ 12 thousand crores to the exchequer was caused in the sale of 21 government sugar mills. The bidding process was highly rigged. Further in this process mandatory stamp duty also was evaded amounting to ₹ one hundred crore as per CAG report.

18. Hawala or Hawala scams or Hawala scandals are very old and popular in India. It involves illegal transfer of money --money does not physically move but what one donor gives

reaches the recipient. No banking systems or financial institutions are involved. Rather middle men are involved who are called Hawaldars or Hawala operators or Hawala dealers. India has so many Hawala kings, operators and Hawalarackets. Though from time to time the above are caught and money seized, what is seized is negligible compared to the total Hawala transactions. Recently a Hawala king was arrested by ED(enforcement Directorate) in a 2,253 crore money laundering. Neither FEMA (Foreign Exchange management act) nor PMLA (Prevention of Money Laundering act) or any other law enforcing agency is able to control this illegal transactions or money laundering. As per one management expert in a period of sixty years, India could have lost 1.5 trillion dollars in the form of tax avoidance and 40 % of this amount are all Hawala transactions (One US dollar as on April 25$^{th}$, 2018 is ₹ 66.94). Extent of our foreign reserves are affected by Hawala transactions. Just one particular state is reported to have an annual remittances of 23 thousand crores in the form of Hawala money. So one can imagine for the whole country!Hawala transactions are done both by Indians residing in India and also by Indians living abroad. Abroad we have Indians who have legitimately gone there and also illegal immigrants. Illegal immigrants invariably have to resort to Hawala transactions. Further people in foreign countries also involve in Hawala transactions. A wide range of people are involved. By pumping money through Hawala transactions into our country other countries can control a wide range of activities –both criminal and non-criminal. Of course in either case the transactions considered as illegal. Many prefer Hawala transactions for many reasons:

(a) Commission charged for transfer of money is less than the bank transfer

(b) Rapid transfer

(c) Transfer of unaccounted money is possible

(d) Illegal immigrants have no other option as they cannot approach regular banks

(e) Sometimes for foreign currency no commission is charged or even given a higher rate.

## Chapter - 5

# Items (goods) / Real Estate/Land/ Infrastructure development / Disproportionate assets

Illegal dealing with various items (goods) is one common nefarious activity that goes on. A few examples are:

1. A senior politician and his family members were involved in pilfering paddy grains from godowns worth one thousand crores.
2. In a particular state a manufacturing company of low-ash metallurgical coke involved in fraudulent purchases and sales to 29 companies. The company possessed highly inadequate equipment, manipulated all accounts, diverted funds and evaded tax. The scam amounted to Rs/one thousand crores.
3. A cooperative union dealing with sugarcane has manipulated the figures of production and supply and the account ledgers. The scam amounted to 18.70 crores.
4. In a particular state, recently DVAC and CBI has investigated the illegal manufacture, import,

supply, distribution and sale of Ghutka. Ghutka is a chewable form of tobacco highly dangerous in any form. Government is spending lot of money to create awareness about its consumption and very likely hood of getting cancer and proving fatal. This evil is there in many states. The Ghutka manufacturer was found to have tax evasions to the extent of ₹ 250 crores.

5. Spanning over a long time repeatedly the scam occurred for the fourth time and several persons including a former VVIP were arrested. The modus operandi of the malpractice was to create fake documents showing the existence of large number of livestock—which in fact were not existing. And as these animals have to be shown as being taken care of fake documents have also been created showing the procurement and expenditure towards various items like fodder, medicines and animal husbandry equipment etc., The money required for the above was withdrawn from various treasuries. The swindling is estimated to be of ₹ one thousand crores nearly. While the above scam is highly familiar with the people there is another similar scam which took place in another state. The magnitude of this scam is much less than the above –only 289 crores. The major modus operandi was to overstate the number of cattle to the government, and swindle the money.

6. As the Green revolution technology is a high input agriculture and as our country is vast there is a high requirement for fertilisers and consequently arose a high dependence on

fertilisers from other countries. Any import or scheme related to fertilisers involves fraud—the magnitude may vary. Relatively recently a large scam of ₹ 500/ crores has become a case of investigation. Fertiliser scams of lesser value also have occurred. Losses to the exchequer, increase of expenditure for the farmers and thereby reduced returns from the crop remains a matter of speculation. In yet another fraud a foreign firm has paid a bribe of one million dollars to a relevant official to secure a contract to supply fertiliser to India.

Indian lobbies with respect to different commodities is known. Not only fertilisers, we have to import many other commodities for genuine reasons or because of malpractices in the country. Genuine reasons mean that we really require additional quantities of a particular commodity. Sometimes an artificial shortage is created by the hoarders. To counter act the hoarding the government has to import. Sometimes to offset the high prices import is made. However all these steps taken in public interest may also involve some malpractices.

7. An official body entrusted with the task of distributing seeds of a particular crop to the farmers happened to purchase seeds from two organisations at a much higher price. This caused a loss of ₹ 5 crores to public exchequer. Further at different times there were also reports of purchasing low quality seeds.

8. An oil rich country was once invaded by another country because of which people were suffering shortage of food materials and medicines. To tide over the crisis, on humanitarian grounds

an apex international body sponsored a programme for the country where they can exchange their oil with food etc., from other countries. Our country also has received 8 million barrels of oil. However our VIP's have diverted and sold at least 3 million barrels of oil to an oil company in another foreign country through Indian intermediaries. As the procurement price of oil from the donor country was much less as compared to the sold price to another country a lot of money was made by the Indian intermediaries. Just two persons seems to have received a commission of 1,46,000/ US dollars.

9. Often strategies followed to do a scam can defy your imagination. Once about twenty five exporters from two states have exported two lakh tonnes of Basmati rice. The contingent was originally destined to one particular country. However, midway the contingent was diverted to another country for sale conniving with all concerned with the act. Ignorant of this the original country also has paid the money for the contingent to the exporters! All these amounted to a fraudulent amassing of ₹ one thousand crores. The distribution of the receipts of the money and the manner in which the money was used could not be determined or divulged. Other rice scams also occurred. In a particular place 77,000 quintals of paddy was allocated at a highly subsidised price. But it was found that a large number of fake transactions were done with fictitious names and documents were shown as if the paddy was distributed to the people at the subsidised

price. The paddy was actually supplied back to the state via many rice millers at a highly inflated price -6-7 times more. At least 46,000 quintals out of the initial supply of 77,000 quintals was supplied by the rice millers to the state after processing. As usual this multi crore scam involved many people. In this process many innocent poor people were put to hardships.

10. A foreign firm has paid a bribe of one million dollars to a relevant official to secure a contract to supply fertiliser to India.
11. Death of Netaji Subash Chandra Bose is being discussed till today —nearly 73 years after his report of death!! Of course the discussion is not related whether he is still alive or not!? Had he been alive he would be 121 years! So people have stopped discussion about his possibility of being still alive. However people do discuss about his fortune being stolen/ appropriated. Some people supposed to have seized his fortune of 100 Kg of gold & jewellery apart from considerable cash. Apart from Indians people in foreign countries also attest to this presumption. All the above was supposed to have been donated by Indians living abroad for freedom movement. Fate of the above fortune remains a speculation.
12. A multi-crore scam related to purchase and distribution of pulses was unearthed. The pulses were meant to be distributed for mid-day meal and supplementary nutritional programme for school children and pregnant women. There was both irregular supply and also supply of poor quality pulses. The scam

was supposed to have occurred in nearly 30 districts of the state. Total scam was worth ₹ Seven hundred crores.

13. In a particular town in a particular state ₹ 7 crore scam occurred in the PDS (Public Distribution Scheme). More than 30 thousand quintals of food grains instead of being taken to government godowns was diverted to open market for sale. Mainly the items included wheat, rice and sugar.
14. A large number of officials both at village level and at higher level were involved in the fraudulent purchase of solar lamps. The scam is worth ₹ 20 crores. However this is considered as small as another scam in the same state has occurred of ₹ 2,600 crores in the purchase and installation of solar lamps.
15. Some firms have cheated a public sector unit of ₹ 464 crores citing the reason of exporting of gold to a foreign country. Instead of exporting they sold the gold in that particular country doubling their profits. Malpractices involves submitting forged documents and sales receipts.
16. Huge losses to state exchequer has occurred because of giving contract to a firm to supply surgical gloves and other disposals at much higher prices to various hospitals. Another scam involved at least 18 medical products by a particular hospital causing huge losses to public exchequer.
17. In just one year fraudulent purchases of seeds, bio-manure, vegetables etc., by an official body caused a loss of several crores to the current exchequer.

18. Large scale embezzlement –several hundred crores —from funds allotted to ambience development by constructing many statues, many monuments etc., was initially reported. However later some estimate this scam to be of 40 thousand crores.

19. Several officials were charged for irregularities in procuring gifts—meant to be presented to foreign dignitaries—of a poor quality and that too at inflated prices. Many such purchased gifts were re-evaluated to know the true value of those gifts which confirmed the above irregularity. (Among our dignitaries occupying high positions there has been a considerable variation. Different people have taken gifts presented to them to different extent to their homes while demitting their offices).

20. An official body was given the task of purchasing different pulses for further distribution through PDS. Due to manipulation the public exchequer was supposed to have lost ₹ one crore per month!

21. An official body was under scanner for misappropriating paddy grains. This mis-appropriation occurred four times and the value of the four scams was ₹ 40 crore, ₹ 2.6 crore, ₹ 5.6 crore and ₹ 17 crore. Both officials and rice mill owners were involved.

22. CBI raided three cement godowns of an official body along with a construction company. The store keepers of the godowns were making wrong entries of the number of truckloads of cement received in their registers for a long time. Scam money is speculative.

23. The Palmolein Import Scam / Palm Olein Case, refers to the alleged irregularities in the import of 15 thousand tonnes oil by a particular state from a company located in a foreign country. Officials have not apparently invited any tenders but arbitrarily selected the company. Company charged a much higher price than the standard market price. This arbitrary order caused a loss of more than 2.32 crores to the public finances.

24. Since quite some time in the recent times we are facing the situation of sale and purchase of a wide range of Chinese goods. These goods are preferred by Indians as they are cheaper. How much of these items are legally imported and how much are smuggled is a debate. However the fact is there is a large availability and sale of Chinese goods in the country. Though not cheaper —maybe even costlier —many imported goods are sold in our country. Here again the same question arises. How much of this legal and how much is smuggled? India was not self-reliant with respect to many goods –particularly quality goods. Hence since Independence we had been purchasing goods "Made in USA, UK, Germany, Japan, Korea, Taiwan etc.,". Even today we purchase foreign goods and smuggling is a known fact starting from small items to gold. Smuggling involves many people. India also legally import so many goods from drugs, food items to defence equipment. And any import can become controversial. Smuggling of so many goods particularly gold, antiques and so many other goods, drug trafficking, human trafficking are reported from time to time.

Customs and border security people sometimes do catch. Smuggling tales place from either side; that is from India to outside and from outside into India.

The most commonly counterfeited and smuggled goods are tobacco, cigarettes, electronic items, gold, machinery and parts, alcoholic beverages, auto components, fast-moving consumer goods and mobile phones. As per KPMG in India's analysis on UN COMTRADE data for years 2012-16, the average annual smuggling of electronics is around Rs 3,430 crore.Similarly, the average smuggling of gold for these years is Rs 3,120 crore, and machinery and parts Rs 5,913 crore. The percentage penetration of illicit trade in the cigarettes market increased from 15% to 21% over the years 2010-15. Factors like higher taxation rates, availability of cheaper alternatives, lack of awareness and lack of enforcement mechanisms are key factors that drive illegal trade in India.

24. There were many reports of people making money by giving contracts to people. Sometimes these contracts are taken by the high profile people themselves or someone on their behalf. In some situations the contracts are given to non-existing individuals/organisations or individuals /organisations temporarily created to assign the contract. Contracts involve a wide variety of goods and services. Accordingly beneficiaries and the amount of benefit accrued varies.

India has only 2.4 % of world's geographical area but has 18 % of world's population. Even in the 2.4 % one has to deduct areas unfit for human habitation. So the area for the 18% population further decreases. In terms of absolute numbers we are 134 crores plus. Hence land has become very precious. Further in view of skewed development of regions cost of land in certain places is too high. Because of skewed development and selective intra-migration density of population also is very high in certain places. It is becoming difficult for us to maintain the recommended forest area and area for agriculture. Selling the farm land for infrastructure development is far more profitable than doing farming in some places. Because of unimaginable increase in the price of land –particularly in urban areas and close to them—many have become rich honestly by selling away their landed properties. Of course they might have evaded tax on their income from selling the lands. As the money value was different in olden days and in recent times and as there had been an unexpected boom in the real estate prices, naturally the value of scams vary and have to be accordingly viewed. Say for example, the value of one acre of land or one house or apartment now is vastly different from what it was 50 to 60 years back! Of course this again varies from place to place. As the market prices can be very high there is a vast scope for scams in the real estate business and infrastructure development for many. Misappropriation of funds in construction works is common. Problems is not just of misappropriation but also of poor quality of construction work whose consequences can vary. Several examples/ cases are mentioned here, but the actual number of cases can be much higher:

1. Sixteen thousand acres of prime land belonging

to the public sector was arbitrarily given to a few families for their own business ventures on long lease for a paltry sum. This caused a loss to the national exchequer of Rs two lakh crores. Further even when the lease period was over lease was renewed to the same people again for a paltry sum.

2. A contract which often people discuss is the collection of money at tolls on high ways. People are totally ignorant: regarding the agreement between the contractor(s) and the government; total amount of transacted money; toll collected till date and for how much more time toll will be collected etc. No media or investigative journalist gives any information on these matters. People keep discussing but no one takes the risk of filing an RTI. This is the situation with so many other contracts or so many issues.

3. It was shocking to academic community that an academician close to seats of power had managed loans from private and public sector to the tune of 22 crores ( as mentioned in the preface this much money was considered enormous in olden days) and established a shipping company. Subsequently became a defaulter and involved in forgery and falsification of accounts of the shipping company. So many high profile people were involved both from India and foreign countries in helping him for a long time. While his amassed wealth is not known he was supposed to pay taxes amounting to about 9 crores.

4. Once a person with no assets rose to occupy a powerful position and amassed considerable

wealth amounting to several crores. State government was apparently helpful to him. Using his office he has purchased high value real estate, farm lands, factories etc., at a much lower price both directly and on some others name. Some of these assets have been given to his family members.

5. Many reposed faith in the potential and exploitation of solar technology. This faith was encashed in a particular state. Two people have floated a solar energy company and collected money in advance from a large number of people promising them to install solar energy devices/panels and even promising them to make them as business partners. Both individuals –ordinary and influential—and several agencies have invested money. Ultimately it turned out to be a fraudulent scheme and many –even influential people—have lost money. This scam is estimated to be around ten crores. Apparently the opinion prevalent/prevailing is that the scam was detected early in view of the alertness of the investors and the opposition party in the state being strong.

6. Infrastructure in a particular city was to be developed by making many constructions like multiplexes, malls, parks etc. An official trust of the state has given the above task to a private firm which has given a kickback of one thousand crores—1,144 crores as reported in media.

7. A senior bureaucrat along with others happened to revive a defunct housing society by false documents. After revival, the society managed

to get lot of state land allotted to it at a much cheaper rate and thereby made a four thousand crore rupees scam. Several malpractices have been resorted to by several people.

8. A massive land scam occurred in a particular state where more than 1,250 properties and land plots were sold. The above were initially on lease but the lease term was expired. Hence there was no compulsion to sell. In this process thousands of crores of revenue was lost to the state exchequer.

9. More than one big scam was associated with NULM (National Urban Livelihood Mission). When the centre has given 1,078 crores of rupees to construct houses for the urban homeless, NULM has constructed only a tiny number of houses—208, while the mission was to construct 9 lakh houses. This has resulted in many states and union territories not having even a single house and some having a countable number of houses. Another scam was pertaining to the development of various skills and training programmes for young people and provide them career placements. Three different NGO's in a particular state were successful in getting 5 crores from NULM. What actually happened was only false claims were made. Either candidates were not trained but fake documents shown or the candidates were deprived of their due training kits and imparted poor training. No placements were given to any one of them. NGO's initially claimed the money with the promise of imparting training and placements to 1200 youth. But all were deceived. In olden days number of NGO's

were countable. But subsequent mushrooming of NGO's till today is something to be pondered over. It is suspected that starting an NGO is a money making / self-employment scheme and has attained or is going to attain the status of one of the most fraudulent activities. CAPART has already declared that vast number of NGO's are bogus. India is supposed to have 31 lakh NGO's i.e. approximately one NGO for every four hundred plus people of the country. ! Stated in another way their number is double the number of schools, 250 times more than the number of government hospitals and so on. At least 833 NGO's have been black listed by the government. We do not know how much money they had already made by then. So CAPART observation maybe right. In general almost all NGO's fabricate documents of donations/income—expenditure statements. Sometimes donors also can be mischievous. They demand from NGO's receipt for more money than what they have donated or may demand a cut from their donations and NGO's oblige. Subsequently NGO's adjust this difference by showing false documents of expenditure. The donors maybe individuals corporate and governmental organisations apart from foreign sources.

10. A building contractor has collected 55 crores of rupees as advance from people promising them individual apartments. Subsequently neither the contractor has neither given the apartment nor returned the money. Rather he sold away the original plot to somebody else.

Nothing could be done and investors continue to struggle.

11. Once a particular government was decided to supply water to people in areas where there was water scarcity with the help of tankers. The contract was given to some private people for the purchase of 385 stainless steel tankers and do the needful. The award of this contract was a fraudulent one and has turned out to be a scam of ₹ 4000 crores. So the exchequer lost this much amount.
12. In a particular state 65 acres of land was acquired from farmers and given to an industrialist to manufacture bicycles on a lease of 90 years. Industrialist did not manufacture the bicycles but sold away the land to a trust to a prominent person.
13. Once the office of CAG made a startling revelation. It stated that three private power distribution companies in a particular place have manipulated so many details of the consumers and acted in so many ways which cause huge losses to the consumers. All these amounted to a scam of Rs / eight thousand crores.
14. A particular state incurred a loss of Rs four hundred crores to its exchequer in the illegal granting of contracts for fishing in various reservoirs of the state.
15. A particular state established a development authority to undertake all the relevant infrastructure development in the interest of the region and the common people there. A senior bureaucrat heading the authority was

accused of Rs 200 crores. Considerable amount of bribes and possession of assets were established.

16. A particular state established a corporation for the development of relevant infrastructure and gave land to the corporation. Corporation land was allotted to wrong people and were further allowed to mortgage the land and avail huge amount of loans from various financial institutions including banks. In this process they made cumulatively Rs /Fifty two thousand crores without any development of infrastructure.
17. Several land scams of lesser value –say of few crores –have been reported from many places across the country.
18. For a locality to be developed an official body has given contracts and suffered a loss of Rs one thousand crores.
19. Due to several malpractices of contractors a particular state has incurred a loss of Rs 100 crores to its exchequer.
20. When a scam occurs with an international grant it spoils the image of the country. Considerable money was swindled from an international grant given for the construction of national highways in a particular state.
21. ASSOCHAM once reported economic losses due to bad conditions of the roads (in other words contractors did a poor quality job) at over Rs thirty thousand crores per year!
22. A big shot happened to arbitrarily give many contracts to individuals and firms providing

services to the communications equipment and components apart from bribes to establish communications. Wealth recovered from his two houses was 3.61 crores. It is suspected that his earnings would be much more.

23. State land meant for industrial development worth Rs four thousand crores was sold for a paltry sum to a real estate developer. Further no fees was charged from the developer as required by law whenever there is a change in the land use pattern.
24. A state body has allotted 36 lakh square metres to promote SEZ (special economic zone) violating all rules. The private promoter caused a loss of Rs forty thousand crores to the state exchequer.
25. A business man floated 17 companies and cheated lakhs of investors amassing nearly ten thousand crores of rupees.
26. Strangely in one of the land scams a defence personal was involved apart from others. Seventy one acres of land acquired adjacent to cantonment and made lot of money by the above.
27. A big shot in a particular state established a trust and allocated prime land of 7,693 square metres to others at a highly subsidised price. This amounted to a scam of Rs twenty two thousand crores of rupees.
28. Huge amount of land was allotted to various categories of people—from wide variety of backgrounds— violating all norms and using discretionary powers of the officials concerned in a particular state. This land was estimated to be of Rs. Four thousand crores at that time.

29. Considerable prime land was sold by a VIP to charitable trusts who in turn have sold it to builders for a huge sum.
30. Two senior bureaucrats were booked for disproportionate assets case. One was possessing ten houses and two shops worth ten crores. Another bureaucrat possessed 50 acres of land, 8 houses, two nursing homes, a medical store, equipment related to building construction and considerable cash. Cumulatively their value is put at 100 crores rupees.
31. State land allotted to sports men to play sports was ultimately sold and made into residential apartments.
32. Two foreign companies were involved in fake water treatment projects and severe malpractices in the operating of water treatment projects. This caused a loss of ten thousand crores rupees to the national exchequer.
33. Retired defence personal are entitled to one plot at a subsidised rate by the government. When plots were allotted it so happened that these were transferred to others on current market prices which are very high. By some manipulations many got more plots. Many seem to have got between two to twenty plots though they are entitled to only one plot! Due to above lot of profits were made.
34. When VIP's/higher officials get involved the land scams value can be very high. In one particular lace it was about Rs. Seven hundred crores.

35. A scam of ₹ 5,887 crores was uncovered pertaining to the construction of an airport. Various irregularities and various categories of people were involved. As the project construction was delayed the cost was nearly doubled. Further a sum of ₹ five thousand crores was swindled during the operation of rehabilitation of slum people around the airport. This can also be treated as an electoral malpractice as there was a serious manipulation of voters list in many places during the rehabilitation process. Another airport scam also has occurred in addition to above.

36. Apart from airport constructions, constructions of smart cities in the country is another major scam involving thousands of crores of rupees.

37. One of the construction scams pertaining to agriculture and other water uses are irrigation projects. These projects can be of different magnitude. In a particular state during a period of ten years 35 thousand crores of rupees was swindled in the construction of projects. This was calculated to be 50% of the total cost of the project.

38. An expert committee happened to disapprove the purchase of a certain type of aircrafts. However it so happened that in spite of being disapproved the same aircrafts were purchased. It was a two thousand crores rupees deal.

39. When a newspaper company got dissolved it has transferred its assets to a new company without following the required rules. In this process the original shareholders were marginalised. The value of the real estate

transferred to the new company was estimated to be about two thousand crores of rupees. The new company has misutilised the real estate in many ways making money.

40. Law enforcing agencies have investigated 29 ULC (Urban Land Ceiling) cases and booked many land owners, real estate agents and officials of municipal corporations apart from others. This scam is a multi-crore scam involving the above and the government has supposed to have been lost at least ₹ three hundred crores to tits exchequer. The modus operandi involved managing and submitting fake certificates for illegally obtaining land for development in the manner the above wanted.

41. A foreign real estate firm formed a joint venture with a state government corporation to build a high end town ship in 535 acres of land. The firm promised a 25 % equity to the cements corporation. Subsequently another corporation got into the venture and only 6.5 % was given. Yet it was approved. This resulted in an illegal benefit of ₹ two thousand and five hundred crores to the foreign firm. Social elite have purchased 135 villas—officially ₹ 5000/ per square yard as compared to market price of ₹ sixty thousand per square yard causing a loss to the government.

42. Ten persons were booked for cheating the government. They sold a land of 434 acres by creating fake documents and claiming the land as theirs. Two additional scams took place in the same state. A VVIP was booked for illegal compensation for industrial compensation for

industrial land worth over ₹ 100 crore. In the other case farmers were cheated by paying them only a small amount as compared to what they really has to get. Official body acquired 450 acres of land from 106 farmers. It opened accounts in the name of farmers by deception and subsequently withdrew the entire money and paid only a part to them.

43. For a long time a land scam was going on in a particular state. A lot of land was illegally acquired from the government and transferred to others. This scam amounted to ₹ one thousand five hundred crores.

44. Real estate developers along with some other fraudulent people have cheated lakhs of people in their respective state and also residing abroad to the extent of ₹ one thousand crores. Modus operandi was, floating dubious financial institutions offering large interest in a short time, offering incentives to investors to rope in more investors in the network etc. At least a loss of ₹ 150 crores was reported by investors.

45. MNREGA or simply NREGA (Mahatma Gandhi National Rural Employment Guarantee act) scheme faced many controversies across the country. Almost every state which implemented the scheme has some allegations of different types of fraud. In one particular state the scam was high worth ₹ Ten thousand crores which is about 50% of the total allotted money. In another state between 53 to 88 % of money was supposed to have been misappropriated in different districts of that state. This was estimated to be ₹ five hundred crores.

46. Three prime builders of mega housing projects have got their licences granted by officials and VIP's fraudulently.
47. A construction company in connivance with an official from a public finance company secured a loan of nearly 1.4 crores by submitting forged documents.
48. A public financing institute was involved in a₹ 380 crore housing scam. However later it was estimated to be of ₹ one thousand crores.
49. Officials of an housing society were caught in a scam of ₹ 500 crores. Several malpractices were involved.
50. An illegal transaction of land of 6 thousand square yards ended up in a scam of ₹ 250 cores in a particular state.
51. Around 150 to 170 crores of fund allotted to an official for development works was utilised only to a much lesser extent.
52. An official of agricultural department has illegally given 132 acres of land at a throw away price to a private firm. Further there was gross misappropriation of funds allotted to various activities like growing flowers, maintenance of cold storage facilities, training of farmers etc., Apparently to accomplish the above many officials were freshly appointed and the existing transferred.
53. Several officials were imprisoned for 3 to 10 years for involving in several hundred crores scam. An official body related to construction was involved.
54. A large amount of money was allocated for supplying drinking water and an official body

was entrusted with the task of water supplying scheme. Several crores were swindled. Malpractices included, non-laying/ non-construction of canals/pipes in many places i.e. they were shown as executed only on paper. Further those laid were also of faulty design.

55. So many housing scams of few lakhs to few crores have been reported from different parts of the country. It is not so uncommon. Many public financial institutions have granted illegally loans to reality developers through a private financial service as a clandestine mediator. Such loans were unusually massive. As real estate sector is booming occurrence of scams and frauds to some extent or other seems to be inevitable particularly keeping in view the high population of our country. Builders adopt several strategies and malpractices like making false promises to buyers, assuring them high rates of interest for their invested money till they get their building/plot, selling disputed land to the buyers, unduly delaying the execution of projects, diverting the land to other purposes depriving the original buyers etc.

56. A financial scandal related to a hydroelectric infrastructure contract between the Indian government and a foreign company resulted in an alleged net loss to the Indian exchequer of ₹ 375 crores The contract was made for the renovation and modernization of the hydroelectric power stations in different districts of a particular state. Several big shots were involved.

# Chapter - 6

# Defence / Sports / Environment / Religious

As many countries are not self-reliant in defence technology they are forced to depend on imports of various defence equipment. India is one of them. Like in imports of many other category of goods defence imports also are controversial and in view of the cost of defence equipment being very high i.e. the total amount of money involved in the purchase of defence equipment is high naturally it becomes a big issue. Defence scams shake up the whole nation and demoralise the public as they involve lot of money and higher officials both in civil and military sector. Further the need for weapons makes the public think that a war is imminent. Both the general public and in particular the families of military men therefore become nervous. A few examples are mentioned here:

1. Once a fleet of helicopters had to be purchased from abroad. Each one involved in the deal amassed wealth to different extent. According to a foreign executive connected with the deal bribes of approximately ₹ 200 crores has been given to Indian officials. In another case of purchase a bribe of just 18 crores was reported.

2. During a war about 500 of our soldiers have died. To immediately bring them back home 500 caskets/ coffins were purchased from a foreign country at a price 13 times more than the original price. Further these coffins were found to be of poor quality. This costed a loss of 1, 87,000 dollars to our government exchequer. Subsequently government has to replace the wooden coffins with metallic coffins incurring additional expenditure. It sounds very strange to all that our own country —with so many corporate houses and business men and a huge population who carry their dead in coffins— could not supply the above requirement!! And it does not require any big science and technology!
3. In a particular place people were astonished to see items dropping from an aircraft. To their shock they found them to be arms—primarily AK-47 rifles along with ammunition in large amounts. The motives, donors and recipients of the arms remains a matter of speculation. However what is certain is that the crew in the aircraft were of foreign nationals belonging to not one but different nations!
4. An investigation agency posing as an international based company dealing with defence equipment approached one of our VVIP's and big shots and negotiated a settlement by initially giving a token commission of 11 lakhs and the remaining commission was promised later. Investigating agency did the above in a highly pre-planned way and documented the record of the negotiations.

5. A latest generation (at that time) aircraft was developed by a foreign air force. Indian builders got license to manufacture them and so it became a joint venture between India and that foreign country at least for a period of 15 years. A criticism was that the above aircrafts were not a priority for the Indian Air Force as better alternatives were available then. Further as the deal was fixed for 15 years another question that arose was whether this aircraft can remain the aircraft of choice in the future also i.e. for another 15 years. By that time likely better versions can crop up. Another condition was all the aircrafts manufactured are to be utilised in/by India itself and are not meant for export to other countries. India had to invest a lot to manufacture these aircrafts. The total deal was supposed to have involved an expenditure of over ₹ 22 thousand crores. Rest of the questions are speculative.
6. Once a shopkeeper was found selling different items meant for soldiers etc., operating at high altitudes. Apparently those who are eligible to get the above items directly or through defence canteens have sold them in turn to the shopkeepers. The items include clothing, jackets, boots, parachutes etc. Further later it was found that soldiers were receiving various food items whose expiry date was over.
7. A scam of purchasing few hundreds of sophisticated guns from other country had hit the national headlines for a long time and is still being discussed. The foreign counterpart was supposed to have paid a heavy bribe of ₹ 64 crores to senior politicians and defence

officials. Many middle men were involved from either side.

8. A big surprise for the people was /is a defence scam has happened soon after independence. This scam pertains to the purchase of vehicles for the army foreign firm violating prescribed formalities. Of course as on the present day the scam amount is very petty—just ₹ 80 lakhs.
9. For launching specific satellites a high value S-band for commercial exploitation has been sold to a private company at an unimaginably low price overlooking prescribed rules/norms. This case also shocked the nation. The band provides an opportunity to deliver mobile broad band services on a widespread common basis across the world. The venture involved our space scientists /officials and foreign investors. Even CAG faced problems in investigating the case but could finally project a loss of at least of ₹ two lakh crores which is more than the Second Generation spectrum case which was supposed to be of 1.74 lakh crores.
10. Adjacent to a sensitive air force base 3.8 acres of land was illegally transferred to real estate developers. The cost of the land was ₹ 20 crores. A much higher fraud occurred in another state. About 200 acres of land around a sensitive air force base was illegally grabbed by real estate developers. The cost of this land was estimated to be of ₹ one thousand crores. The above two scams are of security concern.
11. An apex body dealing with high tech defence equipment was involved in a scam of ₹ 800

crores. It was a difficult task to investigate the malpractices. Ultimately it was found that the malpractices involved purchases of equipment without calling tenders; without the approval of DRDO (Defence Research and Development Organisation) which is mandatory in some purchases and splitting up of all high value purchases by the higher official to the level of ₹ 20 crores which is the permissible limit of the higher official to order for purchases. Anything more than ₹ 20 crores permission need to be sought by the highest authority. Hence the above stipulation was circumvented by reducing all purchases to the limit of only ₹ 20 crores and ordering them as separate items.

12. An higher official wrote in one of his compilations that over 700 trucks for army were sold by a PSU(Public Sector Undertaking) at costs much higher( 4 times more) than the market rates. It procured these trucks from two foreign firms. At least there seems to have been an embezzle-ment of ₹ 750 crores from government funds.

Unlike in olden days in the present era there is a considerable money in many areas including some sports. Assets of some sportsmen are supposed to be of few hundred crores of rupees. Apart from money there is name, fame and career opportunities if one shines in sports. Paradoxically we also listen that compared to other nations our sportsmen participating in international receive an inferior treatment in many respects. In whichever direction there is huge flow of money or there can be flow of money there is also a flow of scamsters in that direction. Like many other scams sports scams also vary in their magnitude. A few cases are discussed below:

1. An athlete really posed a challenge to scientists, law makers and judges. An athlete was suffering from a congenital abnormality called "congenital adrenal hyperplasia" (CAH) or also called "disorder of sexual differentiation" (DSD). The athlete was living as a female in the eyes of the world and had a female live in partner. Due to the above syndrome she was in a position to rape/indulge with the living female partner! Later the living partner complained to authorities. Though arrested no action could be taken on the athlete. Medico-legal-ethics is really complicated.
2. Female members of a sports team which went abroad complained of sexual harassment by coach. Another incident that has tainted the above tournament abroad was the male members involving with the prostitutes of the host country. Their involvement was photographed and revealed to authorities. It is not uncommon that male sports men or for that matter males in any category when they go abroad may spend some time in night life resorts. For some time sportsmen were advised not to indulge at least till tournaments are over as their performance can be affected. Subsequently in some countries sportsmen were allowed to have their spouses or girlfriends to be with them during the tournament. The question finally to be decided is whether indulgence affects the performance in the tournament?". If so the tournament can be lost and the respective nation also looses.

3. Doping i.e. the use of drugs to enhance performance in the concerned game / tournament is an international issue. In the history of sports this is a later development and definitely by the time authorities became conscious and dope tests devised many might have taken advantage of the drugs. Though the drugs may pose health risks yet sportsmen use them for immediate gains of wealth, name and fame. Even as late as in 2011, 30 to 44 % of athletes have supposed to have used drugs for enhancing their performance. Embarrassingly many times many Indians also have resorted to drugs and got caught by dope tests and got disqualified.
4. Once an athlete won a silver medal in an international tournament and was subsequently found to be a transgender. So the athlete award was withdrawn. Indian counterparts have boosted the morale of the athlete by suitably rewarding. It made many feel that it is only humane that tournaments are conducted separately for transgenders as a part of bringing them into the main stream and give them due dignity in the society.
5. Unfortunately a scam receiving worldwide attention has damaged the image of our country. A large pilferage of Rs 70 thousand crores occurred during an international tournament involving selected group of nations recognised collectively in the world. This tournament was conducted in India. Scam involved many malpractices, fraudulent practices and deprivation of our own participants.

6. All said and done probably nothing to beat scams in cricket. Unfortunate part is in future also scams are very likely to continue. The key words are betting, bookies, spot fixing, match fixing, contractors, middlemen, etc. The game now attracts corporate, politicians and other elite. Cricket has become a mania in our country. It is this mania that is being encashed by many. The game has attained the undesirable status of being called as a scandal or scam and sometimes even crime may occur. Money involved in the game can be of the order of billions of dollars. Court cases, police interrogations etc., are not uncommon with the game. Activities related to IPL (Indian Premier League) scams amounts to several hundred crores of rupees every time it is played. So cumulatively one can imagine. In addition to the above mentioned even players also make considerable money. Even tournaments other than IPL also are involved in money spinning activities. Apart from tournaments an official sports body in a particular state has misappropriated funds to the extent of ₹ 11 crores approximately. The funds were initially allotted for the development of infrastructure was swindled by the members of the body.

---

Environment is of a global concern. Many anthropogenic (man-made) activities cause lot of damage to the environment. All the three major components of the universe—air, land and soil are contaminated/ polluted. Unfortunately like in many other sectors awareness pertaining to environment is not there. Both government and other organisations are spending money to create awareness. Governments also have created Pollution control Boards to tackle the problem. Every year world level conferenceson environment are conducted. UGC (University Grants Commission) has made environmental science as a compulsory subject at under graduate level and we have academic programs in environmental science, environmental biotechnology etc. Unfortunately environmental laws are weak and /or considerable corruption exists in activities concerned with environmental pollution. No polluter or any other person gets convicted or any polluting industry gets blocked—rarely if at all. An inevitable part of science and technology is environmental pollution can be caused accidentally or intentionally. To give an extreme example. Just imagine the stockpile of nuclear weapons. What happens if they get exploded accidentally or intentionally!? A day to day example is many wearing nose masks to protect from air pollution. Even oxygen masks are worn to counteract air pollution damage to the body. There is a big list of environmental issues and all of them need to be critically assessed for their damage potential. India is also concerned with environmental issues like industrial pollution, river and drinking water resources pollution, illegal and legal mining of sand, sand quarrying from river banks, coal etc., loss of biodiversity, air and soil pollution, heavy metal pollution, pesticide and fungicides residues, plastic waste and disposal of several other types of waste, fire crackers, natural disasters etc. A recent report says that 14 of 15 world's most polluted cities are in India as assessed by the amount of particulate matter in the air reflecting the air pollution. Kanpur is supposed to be the most polluted in the above list. How and who all to be held responsible and to what extent and the economic losses are a matter of debate. A few examples are detailed below:

1. To provide relief for flood victims a particular state has allocated funds to the tune of ₹ 17 crores. A person created a fake agency and documented that relief material has been supplied to the flood victims without supplying them. Money so amassed was diverted to private companies. How much of the above money has been swindled is a matter of speculation. In addition to the prime accused many were booked.
2. In a particular state illegal mining—illegal extraction of minerals from sand—has been reported in several places. We have many sand and coal mining barons. The site of mining at a particular place came as a surprise. It occurred very near to railway tracks within a distance of 50 to 150 metres that too mechanical mining. Consequences of such mining are damage to the environment and ecology and increased risk of collapse of the railway track. Sand mining or sand quarrying from the banks of rivers in different states has been reported many times.
3. Because of environmental concern and to make the travel cheaper it was decided to use CNG(compressed natural gas) Of the CNG kits supplied to the running vehicles, 20 thousand kits were found to be fake (inferior quality). The contract was accordingly given. Hence a considerable amount of money was misappropriated.
4. Once the office of CAG has made a startling revelation. It stated that three private power

distribution companies. In a particular place have manipulated so many details about the consumers and acted in so many other ways which cause huge losses to the consumers. All these manipulations amounted to a scam of ₹ eight thousand crores.

5. World's most industrial disaster has occurred in Bhopal, India on the night of December 2nd and 3rd in 1984. The case and consequences are not yet over even after 33 years plus! Industry responsible was UCIL (Union carbide of India Limited) which produces several products. Methyl isocyanate is an intermediate chemical in the production of carbamate pesticides. It has also been used in the production of rubbers and adhesives. As a highly toxic and irritating material, it is extremely hazardous to human health. Acute exposure to very high concentrations may be quickly fatal due to respiratory failure. Methyl isocyanate is a skin irritant and may cause chemical burns upon dermal contact. There is no antidote for methyl isocyanate, but its effects can be treated to various extents depending on the severity of the exposure.Nearly 42 tonnes of toxic methyl isocyanate (MIC) along with other toxic gases was overnight leaked exposing more than 5 lakh people to the above gases primarily MIC. Gas leakage occurred because of water entering into the tank of MIC. As to how water entered into the tank remains a point of serious debate. While the company claims water entered the tank through an act of sabotage. Others say it was because of slack management. No one was really got convicted.

A few employees were convicted for short time and got released. Immediate death toll was put at 2,259. Later death toll — over a period of time cumulatively —was put at 16 thousand. Till 2012 waste disposal process was going on and even in 2014 i.e. 30 years after the exposure to MIC, 1, 20,000 to 1, 50, 000 survivors have been reported to be struggling with serious medical conditions. The concept of "justice delayed is justice denied is not applicable" here also as evidenced by the above facts and the feeling among victims and their families that due compensation was received in time or only inadequate compensation is given. If just one chemical company tragedy is of this magnitude then imagine how a nuclear tragedy would be!?

6. A large scale illegal sand and granite scam occurred in a particular state amounting to ₹ 16 thousand crores. While this is a confession by the government others who invested claim that he scam may amount to around one lakh crores. An officially instituted body has given contract/license for mining to several companies. A large number of officials from various categories were involved.
7. A large scale illegal mining activity involving extraction of iron and manganese was reported in a particular state. The scam estimated to be of ₹ 59,203 crores. About 22.80 croretonnes of manganese and iron was supposed to have been illegally extracted. The mining companies not only illegally got the contracts but executed them also violating all mining environmental and other administrative rules. In spite of miners becoming billionaires they paid poor wages to the labourers and no provision was

made for the displaced poor people. These mining companies were still ahead in committing irregularities. They have evaded freight charges to the railways amounting to 1,874 crores and also evaded excise duty. How can all these be done?

8. For mining scams—of varying value—have happened in a particular state. In the massive illegal scam so many big shots were involved and the scam amounted to ₹ 35 thousand crores. In one major scam officials seized iron ore worth ₹ four thousand crores being illegally shipped out of a port. Another major scam involved illegal transport of 10 lakh tonnes of iron ore worth ₹ two thousand crores. A minor scam involved selling of government land worth ₹ 40 lakhs, by VIP's to a mining company for ₹ 20 crores.
9. A development corporation formed by a state was entrusted with the duties of increasing the financial status of farming and labour community by promoting development of forest based and allied industries. Officers were minting money by preparing fake and forged bills. It was considered as a big scam.
10. Central government has allocated huge amount of money to construct toilets in numerous districts in different states across the country. Only about 60% of the total sanctioned number of toilets were constructed. Money for the remaining has been swindled causing huge losses to the exchequer.
11. Through an official body a particular state was involved in a large scale fake plantation of trees cornering several crores.

12. Overlooking the authorities and farmers a firm has illegally encroached upon 650 acres of forest and agricultural land. Many who have invested –which includes high profile people— were cheated by the firm. The consequences of this encroachment and further actions of the firm were: alteration in route of natural water flow which affected agriculture in the nearby areas; land was fenced and roads were constructed on the land thus making them inaccessible to others; paved the way for illegal land mining.
13. A Solar Energy Company was floated mainly by two people who were self-appointed directors of the company. They collected advance amounts from large number of people and investors by promising them to make business partners and promising the installing solar energy panels to trap energy. But duped most of them. The company adopted many tricks to attract more investors and collect money from them but duped most of them. The fraud was estimated to be around ₹ ten crores. It is said that the scam came to light soon as many investors who lost money were highly influential.
14. Workers in industries suffer from so many occupational hazards. The general feeling is — both in private and public sectors – workers are not duly appraised and protected nor do they have medical insurance.

India with its old civilisationand rich religious culture, of late has become a subject of many controversial God men and their organisations and cults. Instead of confining themselves to religious/ spiritual activities they ramify their activities. They run big business ventures of different goods and services, educational institutions, many ashrams, possess huge financial assets and real estates. They even nourish political ambitions or otherwise try to remain close to politicians. They enjoy a huge following starting from common man to VIP's and VVIP's both within the nation and abroad.

Though only the big shots among the Godmen are known nationally and internationally and become a subject matter of discussion the total number of Godmen/saints in the country are a huge number. In Kumbhmelas (A festival held once in twelve years at four different places, where there is massive gathering of Hindus to take a dip in the sacred river)Godmen/ saints (saadhus) and/or their representatives along with a few associates are given the privilege of separately taking bath in the holy river —called locally—ShahiSnaan. They come to the holy river in a procession and take bath and leave. People stand on the banks at a distance watching the procession for several hours! So you can imagine the number of Godmen/Saints (saadhus) in our country.

Unfortunately, in addition to the above their involvement with women—by force or consent— and other crimes of serious nature also have been proved at least with a few. In the recent times one died while serving a prison sentence and one got a convicted and got released. However one Godman was convicted for a rape and sentenced to life imprisonment while yet another Godman facing several criminal charges was sentenced to 20 years imprisonment. Paradox is, all the controversial Godmen had enjoyed a great following —both nationally and internationally—, reverence and reputation for a long time before they became controversial on one unfortunate day. It is more unfortunate for the nation rather than for the individual

Godman. Only time has to tell how many more Godmen will be landing in trouble and cause embarrassment to the society and the nation.

Apart from the Godmen and their organisations even temples — both old and new — have become controversial in view of money making by so many associated with the temples. Religion is now said to have become a commerce — a big economic activity. As so many pilgrims and other tourists visit these temples these places have become a source of huge economic activity for so many categories of people. In spite of the above many temples and cultural sites, even reputed ones — both inside and surroundings — are poorly maintained. Apparently money from the temples income, HR & CA, ASI( Archaeological survey of India and International Heritage funds from UNESCO etc., are not being utilised properly. The recent move and withdrawal of the decision of ASI to take over Tirupati-Tirumala(Andhra Pradesh) -the richest temple in India has become a subject of debate. The receipts and the assets of the temples are not known for certain. HR&CA(Hindu religious and charitable endowments) department has to really involve in investigations regarding the functioning and assets of the temples and also of the tourists places along with other relevant officials. It is often said that house hold in India have more gold than the Government of India. Next to households temples are a big source of Gold and cash.

Hinduism has a an ancient saying – "Dharmo Rakshati Rakshitah" (धर्मोरक्षतिरक्षित) which means dharma (maintaining values—both worldly and spiritual) protects those who uphold and protect dharma. Hence it is vital that everyone should be concerned with any activity concerned with religion.

# Chapter - 7

# Railways/ Airlines/ Liquor (prohibition)/ Sex

In transport sectors, alcohol and night life /sex, there are scams and malpractices reported from different places. A few are being discussed here:

1. Railways have a differential Tariff for transportation within the country and outside the country. For outside the country the tariff can be three times more. To ensure that it is not for export but meant for only within the country the concerned person /company has to submit the relevant documents. Inspite of the above rules and stipulations several parties have transported iron ore to outside the country i.e.exported. The concerned authorities have either not verified the documents or contented with the incomplete documents and charged them only the domestic tariff for transportation which is one-third of the export tariff. So two-thirds of the money of every consignment was swindled and a loss to the public exchequer. Cumulatively the los was estimated by CAG as 17 thousand crores. But even this is definitely a lesser estimate as at the time of the report the

CAG audit was incomplete. Subsequently the estimates have gone up to 50 thousand crores which is likely to be more correct. Hence it is one of the biggest scam. Being a scam in the public sector one can easily imagine the people involved.

2. Several officers were promoted in railways overlooking many procedures and rules. Even a bribe of 90 lakhs has been reported for getting a coveted position in railways.
3. Railways have the provision of keeping certain quota of seats designated as “EQ” (Emergency Quota) originally meant for VIP’s. However VIP’s as on today may or may not travel by train but by flight etc. Hence these tickets lie unused by VIP’s themselves but can be given for sale to others at higher prices. In this process many officials may be involved. As the country is with a large network of railways the above malpractice can yield a lot of money over a period of time. This has been estimated to be around several crores of rupees.
4. Railways were also involved in a huge scam of at least 50 crores. This has happened as an authorised body of railways has given a contract to a private telecom service to provide connections to about 1, 75,000 officers of Indian railways. Apparently the kickbacks were given by the private telecom authority. It is a surprise that railways area public sector and BSNL also is a public sector and yet the contract was given to a private telecom service.
5. There is an accepted norm that airlines and aviation companies have to give free airline

tickets for inspection officials. Other than for purposes of inspections the officials had been demanding and getting free airline tickets for their personal purposes. And the extent of this demand has gone to an extent where this can be called as a big scam. On investigations it has been found that the inspection officials got 2,750 free air tickets in just a span of three years. Of these only 311 were meant for inspection and the remaining which constitute 89% of the total free tickets obtained were used for personal purposes. i.e. for personal travel not only by the officials but also utilised for the travel of their family members and lower officials assisting the senior inspecting officials.

6. Government employees are entitled for free air travel one in every 2-3 years availing leave and this amount is reimbursed by the government. Ait tickets if purchased directly from the airlines would be expensive compared to the tickets given by the travel agents. These travel agents purchase cheaper air tickets much in advance from the airlines and lure the government employees to purchase tickets from them promising them an additional incentive of free accommodation and sightseeing. The employees as per rules are entitled for only travel and not for accommodation and sight-seeing. So the employees prefer to purchase the tickets from the travel agents. Subsequently travel agents give forged air tickets with higher price — which would be on par with what an employee pays if directly purchased from the air lines. Many senior officials travel in this manner apart from others.

7. Several fake pilots were caught by ACB. These pilots apparently got certificates from different flying clubs at different places without the prescribed formal training.
8. A person got arrested for dubious transaction of ₹ one hundred crores. Fraudulently the person has obtained sensitive aerodrome pass (AEP) for access to all airports across the country.
9. A large number of flying schools were established across the country and involved amassing huge wealth. Modus operandi involved was they projected themselves as no-profit no-loss organisations to avoid any payments to the government though they were earning profits. Government has lost at least ₹ 190 crore revenue.
10. As the consumption of liquor has become very high there is a lot of money in it and all aspects of liquor trade—manufacturing, distribution, granting of licenses, sale, illicit liquor, smuggling of foreign liquor, liquor adulteration have become a source of money. This happens all over the country. Paradoxically governments and others spend lot of money on advertising about the ill effects of liquor consumption (in addition to tobacco consumption) in various forms. In weaker sections and in middle class money is diverted for liquor at the cost of the family welfare. Further after boozing the man may involve in family abuse or even in some crime. Many tragedies /deaths or people going blind have been reported from various parts of the country many times as a result of consumption of adulterated liquor. They are

termed as "Hooch Tragedies". Adulteration is intentionally done. Offenders seldom get punished. Fir the victims either there is no compensation or very poor compensation. In view of ill effects, some governments have banned liquor and introduced prohibition. Is the problem solved?? No! Rather it led to newer problems. So many forming a nexus started selling liquor in spite of prohibition/ some boozers have resorted to spurious liquor and drugs. A startling fact discovered after prohibition was introduced was it became difficult for the governments to run the state as the official revenues have drastically reduced. So one can imagine the magnitude of boozing. It did assume evil proportions. So some governments revoked their decision and allowed free sale of liquor. Unless people drink governments cannot run!! Employees of defence establishments —either civil or in uniform; either in service or retired—get tax free liquor. In view of lesser cost many get used to it. And some who do not have the habit of boozing or boozing very less still purchase their entitled quota of liquor and sell to others at higher price — but less than the market price. So both buyer and seller are happy. Not only liquor all other items also are sold at reduced rates to the defence people and they can purchase them even if they do not require either to simply oblige others or to make money. Thus the government is at a loss.

11. All over the world sex is a multi-billion dollar industry. In India also, being a country with a vast population prostitution takes place on a

large scale. Seldom something surfaces though it is a matter of common knowledge that many nefarious activities are associated with this. Purchase of women, kidnapping of women including female children, female trafficking from different states to other parts of the country and even to other countries, trafficking of women from other countries into our country, involvement of musclemen, middlemen and law enforcing agencies and the miserable plight of prostitutes is a matter of common knowledge. Unfortunately laws related to prostitution are not clear and therefore middlemen make lot of money at the expense of paying less for the women offering services. Similarly so for pornography. The way women are exploited for prostitution they are also exploited in pornography.

Further the men who are involved also may run into trouble and remain under fear as the laws are not clear. However government spends lot of money on AIDS awareness. Neither money involved nor money amassed by brothel owners and others gets reported authentically but only as rumours. Brothel owners can come from a wide variety of backgrounds and so also the customers. Apart from well-known ear marked areas for this activity(red light areas) so many other shelters like lodges, business and private establishments are utilised to run this activity. Rarely something emerges. Once a sex scandal in a business establishment hit the headlines in a particular place. Since this activity is very much associated with liquor, narcotic drugs, performance boosting drugs, condoms etc., there is a lot of scope for malpractices and making money in addition to the main activity. Further in some places secret cameras are fixed and the videos are marketed of the activities.

Sex abuse is often reported in shelter homes, social welfare hostels, orphanages etc.

# Chapter - 8

# Digital/ Cyber Crime

## 1. Facebook—Cambridge Analytica Ltd. Scandal and its implications to India

Of late we had been talking about Digital India, Digital Economy, Digital World, Cashless Transactions, Online Transactions, Smart Phones, Apps, Facebook, Twitter, Google etc., The way nuclear energy or for that matter a blade or a knife can be used both for peaceful purposes and also for destructive purposes or crime, the digital technology can be used for creating havoc. Both in India and abroad people have been / are becoming vulnerable. It appears if immediate steps are not taken digital technology can lead to several scams and scandals. In fact people are already living with a sense of insecurity, vulnerability and lack of privacy. Their feelings are not unfounded but are formed as a result of so many reports in India and abroad.

European Union is responsible, visionary and committed to its citizens in enforcing a General Data Protection Regulation (GDPR) from May 2018. It is mandatory under GDPR rules that companies or any association working in the European Union (EU) must get consent to collect personal information. Otherwise done they can be subjective to punitive action. As it is possible for an individual or an organisation to collect, store or process or exploit large amounts of information of the people in the country and even from other countries. A company exposed the personal information of millions of people in US and beyond but did not inform the data breach to the people concerned. Rather they were trying to gain time to take steps to cover itself. GDPR framers are visionary enough to say that the rules apply not only to organisations located within the EU but also to those located outside of the EU in case they offer goods or services to, or monitor the behaviour of EU citizens. This is an outcome of the Cambridge Analytica Ltd. — Facebook massive data mining scandal. Because of GDPR many could file cases against Google and Facebook and also Instagram and WhatsApp which are owned by Facebook. So one can imagine how fast they were to take steps! Is our country prepared accordingly and effectively?

We do not know as yet with accuracy to what extent and how Indian citizens are affected as estimated by our own analysts. Facebook is supposed to have nearly 250 million users in India—20 million more than the USA— and at least half a million Indian Facebook users are affected by data breach/ leaks. People install so many apps in their devices. Because of the installation of the app termed "this is your digital life", Indians have been affected. Cambridge Analytica Ltd which got all the data indulging in massive data mining and subsequently critically analysing it seems to have played a big role in the election campaign of Donald Trump in 2016 who became president of USA. In return the company seems to have received six million dollars.

Some of the parameters collected by the agency were —gender, age, relationship status, ethnicity, health and political views. In spite of indulging in heavy commercialisation company was projecting themselves as a non-profit organisation! Cambridge Analytica Ltd seems to have involved in 44 USA political races in addition to playing a role in the leaving of UK from the European Union (EU)—BREXIT campaign. Regarding the role of Cambridge Analytica Ltd criminal investigations have been initiated in different countries.

Further the agency was also involved in many other countries including India which many people do not know. During the 2010 assembly elections in the state of Bihar Cambridge Analytica Ltd was supposed to have done a critical electorate analysis making use of Facebook users who have installed apps. It is rumoured that a major Indian national political party is a client of Cambridge Analytica Ltd. The company seems to have prepared analysis for the elections in the recently concluded Karnataka Elections and Chhattisgarh & Madhya Pradesh assembly elections which are due in 2018. Of concern to all the political parties and the general public is the report that Cambridge Analytica Ltd has made an analysis for the next LokSabha Elections in 2019. How can they do all these? Are our natives involved or not? It is very likely that many parties may wish to become clients of this company or otherwise try to access the data by all means. Even Cambridge Analytica Ltd may directly or indirectly may sell the analysis to political parties in India for a huge sum. Most of the above is confessed by the CEO of the Face book agency itself. And the number of Indians affected may increase if due steps are not taken. An immediate assessment is required not only with respect to foreign agencies but also with respect to our agencies and those who connive with the foreign agencies. Hacking and Breaches had been occurring and are in fact increasing with time. Our country being a very populous country number of people affected can be very high. Further it needs to be known as to what type of data is leaked and to whom all it is passed on and how the same was exploited or would going to be exploited by the existing and future data leaks. Who all are involved? Not only Facebook those who can have access to your personal data can be many. Say for example, Banks, Insurance companies—both medical and non-medical— and other business establishments which solicit your personal information.

It seems in UK in addition to Facebook about thirty organisations have been seriously investigated for unauthorised use of personal data both for political and commercial purposes. In India also many such organisations may crop up either independently or in collaboration with foreign agencies.

We do not know how in our country any strategy as above was/is used /being used by our politicians or corporates. One well known strategy of our country termed "Electoral arithmetic" pertains to the data collection of population of various social groups in different electoral constituencies. Accordingly the political parties select the candidates for contesting and forming alliances. Apparently information on political leanings of the people in the various constituencies also might be collected or it may be done so in future. In fact in our country many organisations conduct pre-poll surveys and publish the likely outcomes. Whether they are presently using any illegally obtained digital information of voters is not known. In any case it is likely in future and political parties may be said to have done 'digital campaigning".

Our agencies in addition to others make use of specialists called psephologists who specialise in predicting electoral trends. This science is called "psephology". In west the terms "psychometrics" is used to the study of voters inclination and accordingly voters are targeted.

Just imagine if any above such analysis is used for splitting a state into two or more states? In our country any analysis as above is likely to increase electoral corruption during the pre-election phase and increase in post-election promises for candidates/political parties to win.

**2. Aadhaar Card Data Breach**

A grand initiative has been taken in 2009 by the Indian Government to create a data base of the entire population of India and created an office of Unique Identification Authority of India (UIDAI). The process involved biometric information of the individual finger prints of all the ten fingers and thumb impression and iris scan of the eye in addition to the photo and general details of the person. Being a country of huge population this exercise was called as "the biggest social project on the planet." and "the most sophisticated ID programme in the world." Based on the above everyone is issued a card bearing a 12 digit unique number along with the photo, complete name and also indicating the gender, date of birth and address and QR (quick response) code. This card is to be treated as a multipurpose National Identity Card, or Unique Identity card (UID Card) and in popular terminology is called as "Aadhaar" card. Now the Indian Government has a large data base of its population. As on April 2017, 1.14 billion Indian people got their ID number.

Strangely for reasons unknown the process does not demand the signature of a person which is a must for voter identity cards and income tax PAN (permanent account number) cards etc. Of course as India still have people who cannot sign are allowed to use their thumb impression.

Aadhaar card is used by the citizen to open a bank account, buy a SIM card for the mobile phone and as an identity verification of the individual at various places etc.

There is an enormous scope at various levels for leaking the Aadhaar card data base of the individuals—rather all the 1.14 billion people! In fact even during the initial execution the program was criticized for violating people's privacy and exposing personal information and now such criticism/apprehension is nearly total. As to how all the data will be exploited we have to wait and see. Reports of money stealing because of identity theft of Aadhaar card and pin numbers of bank debit cards were there. That data has been breached/leaked has been reported authentically in some news media. The Aadhaar card data can be sold to others who in turn can sell to some others and so on. A news media has reported that one can buy Aadhaar card information for ₹ 500 / and it takes only ten minutes for the whole process of giving the information. It is speculated that the information has been sold to at least one lakh service providers. It seems many are offering / selling access to Aadhaar card information. It is also reported that one can even print fake Aadhaar cards using specific software technology with any unique 12 digit number one wants. At the rate of Rs/500/ per card it is probably not a big money for multinationals or corporates coming together and getting the information of all the 1.14 billion individuals of India to the extent given in the Aadhaar card.

Of course all the above is totally denied by the authorities of UIDAI and asserted that Aadhaar card details are safe and secure. But people have their own apprehensions. Because leaking of information from Government offices or private establishments is a common thing that can happen.

### 3. WikiLeaks and implications to India

Another organisation perceived as dangerous was "WikiLeaks" (Do not confuse between WikiLeaks and Wikipedia. They are totally different.). WikiLeaks also claim to be a non-profit organisation which cannot be convincing to people. It is involved in publishing secret information, data leaking, etc. which it gets from various sources. Though relatively recently established —in 2006—apparently because of digital era it is supposed to have an enormous data base of about ten million documents pertaining to various countries in the world. It did leak so many documents all of a sudden related to various crucial issues, crimes, wars, scandals etc. Apart from serious national and international issues it also leaked personal information of many like credit card numbers, insurance policy numbers, information about individual's health care, passport details, family particulars, employment records etc. India also is one of the countries about which lot of information has been leaked, like black money holders, Swiss bank accounts, Political information, corruption, and many others as mentioned above. We do not know how they got access and since when they had been accessing. It is definitely embarrassing to the country.

**4. Miscellaneous.**

(a) In 2016 hackers got 57 million records of both drivers and customers of "Uber" in USA. The data included, names, email addresses, mobile phone numbers, driver's license numbers and their names. If this happens in USA it can happen in India too. India has Uber. Further we have "Ola" also and the same hacking can happen with both in our country too. Whether it has already happened but not leaked we do not know.

(b) There is a tremendous increase of usage of smart phones in India. It seems about half of the internet traffic originates on mobile smart phones and data breach occurs from these individuals. This is in addition to the data breach because of the app mentioned above.

(c) Occasionally we keep listening to hacking of our government organisations by people within or from other countries. Demolishing the others computers by introducing computer viruses is also reported. Cybercrime has been used in so many illegal activities internationally and therefore it has all the possibilities of occurring in India.

(d) A recent south Indian movie—very likely to be dubbed or remade in other languages too— has induced lot of discussion both among general public and computer professionals about Digital/ Cybercrime /cyber terrorism. Being a movie definitely there can be some exaggeration of the depiction but it does not seem to be totally unfounded. That is how people are thinking. Even highly educated people who know about the use of satellites for monitoring, and what is mentioned above(1-3 and 4 a to c) and occasionally what is projected as science fiction coming true feel that, if not to the same extent shown in the movie at least to considerable extent such things can happen creating problems for people. Many say that it is safe to use a basic model mobile phone rather than a smart phone.

According to the movie, one's money from banks can be withdrawn or deposited without ones knowledge or intervention in any way; all conversations and messages from smart phones can be tapped; one's data from Banks ATM machines can be tapped; EVM's (electronic voting machines can be tampered; possibility of satellite monitoring of one's movements; fitting of microphones on one's body with or without consent by the help of which information of others can be tapped; stealing of hand and finger prints; fitting of CCTV cameras and monitoring or through already existing CCTV cameras; ( In fact fitting of secret cameras in ladies dressing rooms of garments shops and in lodges is well known and is feared by public. In fact with a secret camera a Governor's activity was videoed and put on YouTube and was watched by many Indians. Indians going abroad in particular officials must be careful in their residential places. Further people acknowledge fitting of cameras in pens and buttons); use of sophisticated wrist watches by the help of which one can do so many things etc. Apart from the above sophisticated technology routine data leaks —which general public are very familiar—are also shown. For example, when we give any material for Xeroxing the Xerox man takes an additional copy for himself and sell the same to others and that is how lot of data is leaked.

(e) Recently, a serious alert was given to delete 180 apps from the smart phones which can prove dangerous. In 2017, it seems Google has announced that it has removed as many as seven lakhs bad apps from Google Play Store.

(f) Introducing QR (Quick Response) code in students transcripts and other certificates makes the institutions keep a complete record of information of the students (it is rumored that particularly private institutes are interested in such a exercise). Of course QR is also projected to protect students/institutes to know their exact marks obtained in their exams and naturally any change will be subjected to investigation.

(g) So far, around 900 cybercrime cases are registered in the state. Of these, 30 per cent are phishing frauds (Telangana State). Phishing is the fraudulent practice of sending emails purporting to be from reputable companies in order to induce individuals to reveal personal information, such as passwords and credit card numbers."Most of the phishing scams take place in rural areas where conmen loot money after obtaining the PIN and CVV. In 2016, 713 cyber fraud cases were registered in the state, according to the NCRB data, and they were related to personal vengeance, sexual harassment, and phishing. The CID is now focusing more on training and drafting standard operation procedures for cybercrime units in the state.

(h) Not only Indians suffered because of others, but even others suffer because of Indians. Over four years more than fifteen thousand victims in the United States lost "hundreds of millions" of dollars to the sophisticated call center scam, and more than 50, 000 individuals had their personal information misused. The money was supposed to have been routed through call centers in India back to the ringleaders in eight states.

(i) Very recently a private co-operative bank in a particular city was hacked and cheated of 94 crores and the money was transferred to foreign accounts. Technology involved breaching the firewall in servers that authorize ATM transactions. Subsequently hackers were able to create a proxy server which does not differentiate between genuine cards and fake cards. Hackers have duplicated VISa and RuPAY debit cards and used them to make transactions and attacked the ATM switch to verify them. Nearly 15 thousand such fraud transactions were made.

# Epilogue

An old saying – "everything is fair in love and war". As on today probably we can modify the above quote as "Everything is fair in everything"! "Everything is fair in all endeavours". Not only in love and war but also in politics, Business, administration, academics, International relations and even day to day human relations ——whatever happens everything is now being considered as fair/ justified. ! What a pathetic situation!? This is probably justified by another saying—" Man's capacity for self-deception is enormous". Hence one tries to justify everything. Those who are objective, cherish values and concerned for the society and the nation are decreasing with time. So it is high time that every one of us undergo a thorough self-introspection and transform oneself and become capable of analysing the state of affairs in all integrity and strive towards perfection in the long run.

In Netherlands and Norway it seems many jails/ prisons are getting closed as there are no criminals! In our country the prisons are cramped. And the reality is we are in extreme shortage of prisons but we are not feeling it because a large number of criminals are not caught and convicted!

Remember what is mentioned in the preface. "It is just a tip of an iceberg". So do not underestimate the gravity of the situation in the country. If this statement is right what comment on various law enforcing agencies and official watchdogs? Are they so indifferent to most of the wrongs happening in the country!? How and why? It is worth repeating that there is absolutely no scope for underestimating the gravity of the situation in our country. Future can be any unpredictable.

Dear fellow citizens, we have to be alert, vigilant, diligent, coherent and honest with a mission and vision in the interest of our own security. We should not be penny wise and pound foolish.

Dear fellow citizens, remember "prevention is better than cure" and"A stitch in time saves nine" and "Better late than never". Already we have lost lot of time. So we should acquire the required knowledge and have total commitment to prevent ills in time. It is true that it is a gargantuan task and we should not be demoralised and become cynical. That leads to indifference and inaction which will only accelerate the pace of deterioration. As the BhagwatGeeta says even practicing a little of virtues can save you from great fears. So imagine in case we can practice virtues in a large measure! Evils can spread from anywhere. Hence we should be cautious and take timely action as required. Just one example is probably what is mentioned under "Digital/ Cyber Crime". We should be highly self-introspective and self-disciplined and not self centered, self seeking, self deceptive and self indulgent. No need for utter self denial but only for due assessment in the interest of the society and the nation.

From the subject matter presented in the text some corollaries and suggestions naturally emerge and are mentioned here to facilitate a beginning for deliberations by a large number of people across the country.

1. Form self-help groups and keep interacting constantly. These groups should keep a record of — as much as possible — of what all that goes on wrong. When a large number of self-help groups come together from across the country to interact the outcome is very likely to be fruitful. Members of the self-help groups should come from wide variety of backgrounds and human rights activists. As people from wide variety of backgrounds are involved in malpractices good Samaritans from all these backgrounds should become members of these self-help groups particularly those who held or holding responsible positions.
2. People should have access to adequate, authentic and classified information. This is not easy as complete information may not be available from the media. Even a single law enforcing agency may not have but have to pool up the information from various law enforcing agencies to have a complete picture.
3. Archives must be carefully preserved but not destroyed by all offices and media. In fact many archives are preserved and that it show old cases keep getting published in media or raked up by some politicians and high officials. People should demand a copy of the archives to be kept in all major libraries in the country. People should have as much information as possible to chalk out further course of action. A high level of consumer /client awareness is a must in all sectors. It may not be possible for everyone

to do everything not everyone can be a whistle blower. Not everyone can file an RTI or PIL. As big shots can be involved in scams etc., people should be cautious in reacting. Therefore people need to be identified who can do the required job.

4. There is a saying. "Why to break the law when there are so many legitimate ways of being crooked"? People should understand that many are able to do malpractices because of loopholes in our laws, rules and regulations. Every sector suffers from this. Hence we should identify the loopholes in our frame work of laws, rules and regulations and plug them effectively and without any ambiguity. In fact in no law or rule or regulation there should be any ambiguity. It should not give any scope for an alternative interpretation.
5. In all sectors men in the chairs enjoy legally some discretionary powers. If one questions them it cannot stand in court of law. Can these discretionary powers be removed / minimised/ altered? The public opinion that prevails is that discretionary powers are used in general only for vested interests. Of course things can go wrong with anyone, from common man to VIP's and VVIP's.
6. Many projects funded by international agencies in different sectors had become controversial spoiling the image of the country. Extent to and manner in which foreign aid can be swindled can vary. An extreme case appeared in newspapers long back. A particular country received a foreign aid for its welfare/ developmental activities. It seems within 12

hours the entire money was back in a foreign bank! While this is an extreme and seems incredible, small portions of the aid landing in foreign banks no one tries to distrust. There is another dangerous opinion that prevails. Foreign corporate /agencies do give big kickbacks in some deals and themselves reveal it at a later date at an opportune time!Why? A feeling is they want to create chaos in the country and/or cause downfall of the existing regime. To what extent the above is true is a different story. But the fact that such opinions are expressed indicates that some do think and correlate things like that. In such a way their mental balance is lost because of the scams, kickbacks and other events following. So we should be experts in international relations and affairs. UN organisations publish so many documents related to underdeveloped, developing countries and developed countries. People should read them. Whether a country monitors and evaluates itself or not UN organisations often do so.

7. Time taken to investigate a scam and solve can take a very long time. End results can be variable. One extreme is no one gets convicted and no scam money recovered. In other cases a few may get convicted for different periods of time in prison and the extent of money recovered can be highly variable. To what extent victims are compensated or the public exchequer is compensate can be variable and debatable. Why in some cases no one gets convicted though the general public strongly believe that particular person (s) are guilty? You are

innocent unless you are proved guilty in a court of law. If the guilt / scam cannot be proved court cannot penalise anyone. Why so many law enforcing agencies who have revealed the scams and continued the investigation for a long time are not able to prove the guilt? Apparently investigation and documentation of evidences is not adequate to stand in a court of law. Of course the other feeling that prevails is, political interference. Another question that arises is why law enforcing agencies detect, reveal and probe a scam for a long time? Is it out of their commitment to their duties or to justify their existence or there had been some political directive to do so or because of some strong whistle blower(s)? The question becomes relevant because often it is said what went wrong and reported is "just a tip of the iceberg"!

8. Since electoral expenditure is one of the root causes for many malpractices people should seriously ponder as to how electoral expenditure can be minimised to the lowest possible.
9. One reason which general public say as valid. Not because of greed but even for a minimum decent living the amount of money that is required as on today is very high and this amount cannot be met by legitimate sources of income. This is one common justification which people give for them indulging in making money by various and that is how we are forced to acknowledge that corruption is rampant and all pervasive. Apart from the needs of the huge population Defence of the country drains away a large amount of money. How to be self reliant and a power to reckon with to defend our

nation apart from meeting the material needs of the huge population? It is the calibre and commitment of the people in academic sector that is of vital importance in this regard. Hence this sector should never be compromised in any manner. Further people should differentiate between genuine needs, luxury, greed, craze etc. They should regulate their requirements and attitudes accordingly in the interest of themselves and the nation. It is the above needs and weaknesses that are often exploited by scamsters.

10. One wrong person in a key post can subvert the whole system. In our system we have so many key posts. Therefore all concerned — starting from voters to higher ups —must exercise due caution while appointing persons to key posts. Further they should be constantly monitored and evaluated effectively. We require numerous faithful and competent watchdogs in our system.
11. People and social custodians should become extremely alert and assertive regarding Digital/ Cyber Crime.
12. There is nothing wrong to be nostalgic and proud of our ancient civilisation. But we should understand the limitations to bask in the glory of the past and come to terms with the present realities and the likely future.
13. A realisation should dawn on us that our country should be self-contained without any friction and a power to reckon with on the globe. A realisation should dawn on us that if we do not sink our differences and work together

with all our might and integrity on all fronts we all would collapse one day—probably never to bounce back again.

14. Total number of cases of malpractices, scams, scandals and their magnitude is such that man power available for investigating them in DVAC, ACB, CBI, CAG etc are not sufficient and are not able to cope up. Equally, if not more true in case of judiciary where a huge number of cases of varying complexity are pending for unduly long periods. It is honestly felt by many that man power available for is much less compared to the cases to be handled.

15. Most unfortunate part is people try to justify rather than condemning corruption, malpractices etc. or taking steps to prevent them. It is shocking to listen to many people's statements justifying, say "After all they are human"; Kon paisa nahinkaatha/ banaata "; uskodekho, iskodekho etc. and try to justify corruption malpractices etc. of their interest if not all! This attitude should change. Quoting bad precedences and justifying perpetuation of corruption is to be condemned.

16. The fact remains that corruption is all pervading. That is it exists in all spheres of human activity. The extent may vary in different sectors and different pockets of India.India has been ranked 81st in the global corruption perception index for 2017, released by Transparency International, which named the country among the "worst offenders" in terms of graft and press freedom in the Asia Pacific region. The index, which ranks 180 countries

and territories by their perceived levels of public sector corruption, placed India at the 81st place.

17. Does the Prevention of Corruption (Amend) Act recently passed by the government-July 26, 2018- is going to stop or at least reduce corruption??

Dear fellow citizens remember Rabindranath Tagore's Gitanjali.

"Where the mind is without fear and the head is held high

Where knowledge is free

Where the world has not been broken up into fragments

By narrow domestic walls

Where words come out from the depth of truth

Where tireless striving stretches its arms towards perfection

Where the clear stream of reason has not lost its way

Into the dreary desert sand of dead habit

Where the mind is led forward by thee

Into ever-widening thought and action

Into that heaven of freedom, my Father, let my country awake".

# Index